DESTINATION
TENT CITY,
AZ

DESTINATION TENT CITY, AZ

As Told To

Mark Feuerer

coffeetownpress
Seattle, WA

coffeetownpress

Coffeetown Press
PO Box 70515
Seattle, WA 98127

For more information contact: www.coffeetownpress.com

The following is a true story. Names and identifying details have been changed.

Cover design by Sabrina Sun

Destination Tent City, AZ
Copyright © 2011 by Mark Feuerer

ISBN: 978-1-60381-109-5 (Trade Paperback)

Printed in the United States of America

This book is dedicated to the multitude of men and women who are working hard to atone for their bad decisions.

CHAPTER 1

April 11, 2009: Going to Prison

The next twenty-four hours will be anything but a dance in the street. In fact, I feel like stepping out into a foggy, busy street and closing my eyes. It's barely daylight as I climb into my mother's 2007 Honda Accord—and yes, forty-six-years-old and mom is carting me around like a teenager—dressed in black tights, a t-shirt, and a pair of my nephew's old jeans. A surge of anxiety fills the emptiness in my stomach, where breakfast should be residing; lack of appetite has given it the Heisman stiff arm. Eating or drinking anything was not an option anyway—what goes in must come out—and much to my surprise given my state of mind, I actually had the forethought to realize where "out" was to take place in relation to where I was going.

Any chance that the gas pedal will stick and we'll speed uncontrollably into oncoming traffic? If it weren't for the zero survivor rates of head-on collisions, I would silently hope for such devastation. I love my mother, I do. She's dealing with this as best she can. And the oncoming traffic shouldn't be victimized—they have no idea why I would think such sadistic thoughts. So I just try to clear my mind. Everything seems blurred and incomprehensible. What was supposed to be my last night of restful sleep for a while gave way to tears and thoughts of the uncertain future, the result of one crushing incident several months ago. The anticipation and anxiety that had been building for months was finally about to be faced head-on.

My short list of allowable supplies consists of a book, sweatshirt, two towels, a plastic flashlight, an alarm clock, my watch, and $40 cash, only some of which I have in a plastic grocery bag this dreadful morning. Sounds like a list made for a camping trip and that, in some twisted way, is fairly accurate. Mind you, it's not for a lack of nice baggage that I tote my goodies in a Safeway bag. Coach or D&G have no business going where I'm going. Did I mention I'm headed to prison? Humiliated, ashamed and dirty, I am silent, as is Mom, during the whole thirty-five minute trip. Partly because it's 6:15 a.m., but mostly because there isn't much to say to your daughter as consolation before her first full day and night in Tent City.

CHAPTER 2

As we pull up just outside the intake door, we are both silently thinking that the jail was easy to find. There are people standing outside already, prepared to self-surrender at 7 a.m. It's taking every ounce of energy in my body to pull my legs and torso out of the car to join them, but what options do I have? The last chapter of this horrible journey begins here. Better to go and get it over with.

"Just leave … I'll be fine," I tell my mother. I am so embarrassed for her to see me go through this. She knows that I've always been the caretaker of the family … the giver. Now it's my turn to ask for help and I think she knows just how difficult that is for me. I sense the fear of those waiting to enter. It looks to be about twenty men and only three other women. The building's exterior, beige with a blue trim around the windows, is crowned with razor wire. As the guards open the doors, we all walk into the building, single file, everyone keeping to themselves. Glancing over my shoulder for one last look at the outside, I see my mom standing outside of her car, watching me disappear. It is as if she is watching me enter kindergarten on my very first day. As I hesitate there for a brief moment, throat and stomach in knots, I imagine what's going through her mind. Like most of the people in my life, she won't know the full truth about this experience until she reads this memoir. I doubt I will ever be ready to freely discuss what happens here outside of therapy.

* * *

Two thousand nine had been a rough year, with the first anniversary of the demise of a five-year relationship with "Lucky," a skinny workaholic who found more ways to create illusion and deception than Copperfield. Still loyal to the end, I hung on to his every lying word until he ultimately couldn't hide his true character any longer. When I began to discover the trouble he took to hide his other life, I was left feeling stranded, gullible, and amazed that anyone could be so cruel. To top it off, the struggling economy and my inability to make ends meet were weighing heavily. Being single and living alone is hard. Expensive. Three mortgages (my own, my mother's, and one for some land in the upper Midwest), a car payment, and general living expenses had forced me to get my ass in gear, out of the house and back into working long hours. The stress and depression were making matters worse. There was a day when work fell way down on the list of enjoyable things to do in my life—now it's the only way I can get through the long moments of despair I feel daily.

"Good time" friends were just around for good times. Each family member was swimming in their own little world. I was drowning in mine. No one picked up on my subtle yet desperate need to be comforted. I'm a caregiver—have been my whole life. But caregivers occasionally need to be cared for. That wasn't happening. Desperate to get back among the living, I was actually considering digging up an old corpse ex-fiancé. I was almost at the point of believing the illusion that I could get my life back if I got back together with him. Even though I knew it was wrong. My cell and dialing thumb were in constant motion, in most cases just one press away from compounding the mistakes I had already made. I just needed to take a deep breath and remember, one day at a time …

* * *

November 8, 2009: The Beginning

It's Sunday morning and, as I step out of my door, I'm greeted with beautiful autumn weather. I take a couple of deep breaths; the air has a certain crispness to it that cools my lungs. Arizona, especially this time of year, is vastly different than most other states in terms of scenery and climate variation. Within a two hour drive in any direction from Phoenix, experiences vary from scenic rugged terrain, to the gorgeous colors and cool temperatures of the fall, to the desert landscape of the great Southwest. Pick a day and a direction—beauty awaits.

Stretching, I walk back inside to get the day started. Standard daily procedure—water the outdoor plants, feed the dogs, have a small breakfast. I had tried to make plans with a couple different friends for the weekend, but it seemed everyone was too wrapped up in the duties of the day or just letting their cell phones go to voice mail. I just want to get out of town … take a drive … maybe go to Jerome or Payson. I feel a strong desire to have a companion along—a friendly presence. Stretching my calling circle, I begin dialing the second-tier friendship network. After numerous turn-downs, I decide to take a drive solo to Payson. Convincing myself that this is a much better arrangement, I head off to Church— as I affectionately call it—my favorite local hangout where sins are confessed and forgiven, at least for the day. Pulling up a barstool, back to the front door, I order a beer and ask the hot, thirty-something bartender for a bag of ice for my cooler. It always surprises me to walk into this place at 9 a.m. and see the bar filled with familiar faces, all hunched over their drink, waiting for the morning to hand the day off to the afternoon. The pool table is clear, except for the cue ball and the beer stains, and all of the cues are tucked neatly in the corner rack. Trudy and Darryl are sitting in their normal spots, each quarter-turned to face the other. Alcoholics? Probably, but they're in love and seem happily drunk in Church this morning. Randy, with a cold glass of Bud Light and some loose change in front of him, just stares blankly ahead, occasionally following the bartender's activities with his eyes as if he was plotting to sneak a quick pour from the tapper that separates him from the bar back. To get a reaction out of him is always a challenge, but today he glances over as the bartender sets my beer in front of me. Looking his way, I raise my glass and say "Cheers!" Elbows on the edge of the bar, Randy's right forearm and hand raise up with his glass for a second before he sets it back down again without taking a sip. It's possible he may have smiled just a bit, but I can't be sure. A couple of unknowns round out the census at Church, each moving and saying as little as possible. Morning drinkers are like coffee drinkers—they can't function until they've had a couple, and then you can't shut them up. I wasn't going to stick around to see everyone come to life—I've got a road trip planned and I'm getting excited to start the trip.

Settling in on the idea of driving alone, I begin the one-hour-plus drive. A short stop to fill the tank and pick up the day's essentials—some snacks and a six-pack of Bud Light—and off I go. I can feel the angst begin to give way to the beautiful surroundings. I've made this drive hundreds of times, but today is a bit different. The realization of how small my social circle is begins to overwhelm my thoughts, mile after mile. This sort of aura has its upside—no one else's drama to consume me, no one else's thoughtless favor requests for me to fall victim to. Maybe this is what God intended for me after my long struggles to find a life partner. Already divorced once, my barrier walls have grown tall. After the failed relationship with Lucky, barbed-wire now sits atop.

As I drive on the Beeline Highway, surrounded by one of the most beautiful skylines, I finally settle into the day. Listening to music and downloading CDs onto my truck's on-board computer system, I mouth words of the songs, occasionally letting go of a few surreptitious notes. The windows are down and the sunroof is open. About twenty miles south of Payson, I see an older man with a broken-down bicycle by the side of the road. He's not motioning for anyone to pull over, but I can't just drive by and ignore his obvious predicament. Slowing down to a stop about fifty yards ahead, I walk back and ask him if he is okay and if he needs any help. His story is similar to mine. He has been cycling all day, trying to get to Cottonwood to see his granddaughter. The desire to be around family is apparently strong today. He was willing to do whatever it takes and had faith that his bicycle and adrenaline would make the ninety-mile trek from point A to point B. Now there's a guy who truly loves his granddaughter! I'm not saying he is the brightest bulb in the box, but his ambition is humbling.

My guard is up, but my heart responds to his plight.

After a stern warning that I carry a gun and am not afraid to use it, I load his broken-down bike into the back of the truck and off we go to Payson to find a bike repair shop. While I do have a few guns and enjoy the sport of shooting and the protection it provides, I don't have one with me this day. The man is a Native American, probably in his sixties. Seems harmless enough. He happily accepts the beer I offer up and we begin our idle chatter.

Yes, I know—open intoxicants in a moving vehicle. I certainly don't live by the letter of the law.

Our arrival into Payson is followed by a search for a bike shop. Knowing very well that his trip has been cut short—at least temporarily—and that there is no way he is going to make it to Cottonwood, I ask what his plans are for the remainder of the day. He confirms what I already suspect—he has no money to cover the repair or a place to stay. So I offer—no, insist on—paying for a hotel near the bike repair shop. My six-pack has now turned into a four-pack; when I leave him in the parking lot of the motel, I give him another beer. Saying he is appreciative is probably understating it a bit. Calling me his guardian angel is a probably somewhat overstated. Let's just say that God's intervention has once again been successful. We are both better for the experience.

The couple of hours spent in Payson are fairly uneventful. I people-watch, pretend-shop, and just generally enjoy the ten degree temperature drop. My pleasure in the cool fresh air is accompanied by relief over how I have taken back control of my life. Once again. Finding balance has always been a work in progress. The shifting and swinging of being is oftentimes uncontrollable, and it requires a trip like this to slow down and eventually stop the metronome of life at its midpoint.

Before leaving Payson on my journey back to Phoenix, I stop off for a snack, which turns out to be chicken tenders. After cleaning out the truck and disposing of the empty beer bottles, I am back on the road again—my cooler holding the final frosty beverage.

The start of the drive home is peaceful. Completely relaxed, I am feeling pretty upbeat—happy that I was able to help the roadside bicyclist find a safe home during his journey and satisfied that I have cured the day's wanderlust with this trip. I continue to download CDs, enjoying the weather. A Sunday drive not unlike so many others, allowing me to enjoy the simple pleasures of Arizona's beauty. It doesn't even occur to me that I should have reconsidered getting behind the wheel or at least waited a few hours before heading back. I feel fine and completely in control and safe behind the wheel of my truck. After all, I only had a few beers over a span of maybe three hours. Granted, at 115 pounds, it probably doesn't take much, but my tolerance to alcohol has really never diminished to a point where I would think my weight would become a factor.

I will remember every turn and every stop made this day. Exiting off of the Beeline and heading west on Shea Boulevard just outside of Fountain Hills, I am nearly home. It is approximately 4:30 p.m. I am around 92nd / Shea Boulevard when I see the police lights in my rearview mirror …

CHAPTER 3

Now inside the barren county building, I begin to register the faces of those around me and the silence. I suddenly feel alone, like a teenage girl who has just found out she's pregnant. The unknown has a way of silencing and softening the toughest of crowds. It's only been ten minutes, but already I'm losing track of time. The borrowed Velcro-strapped watch I'm wearing, which is larger than the width of my wrist, only confuses my warped sense of time passing.

We are escorted single file into the intake building and separated, men on one side, women on the other. "All of you," the guard says as he points in our direction, "go in here and wait." This must be purgatory ... and God is deciding how long my time of suffering shall last before sending me into the depths for eternal damnation. Too dramatic... get over yourself.

We are put into the first holding cell with the door left open. I don't want to look up and make eye contact with anyone, but as they say, human nature has a natural curiosity about car wrecks and I'm on the ceiling of one that's flipped, staring out of the broken-out window waiting for someone to notice me. I watch as each male, seemingly from all walks of life, is called one by one to get photographed. It's really beginning to feel surreal. We're next. I watch the first three women, one after the other, dazedly step up to the two foot prints on the floor and, as they gaze straight ahead, flinch at the quick click of the camera. My turn. Stepping to the front, I expect direction but get none. I look straight ahead and, like all the others before me, flinch at the clicking sound. Not that I was waiting for someone to say cheese … it just would have been nice to know what's in store for my immediate future, as in two to three seconds from now.

Mentally, I tag this photo as the beginning of my incarceration. Before it, I was still free to leave and temporarily avoid the inevitable. As the photo taker hands me my new ID with my mug shot, booking number, today's date and date of birth, I begin to think of myself as forever documented as a criminal in some international database. The card slides into my back pocket as I slide into new depths of depression.

Handed a piece of paper, again without so much as a short explanation of what it is, I begin to read. Okay … they're asking me to sign a document stating any medical issues, or requesting that medicine be brought into the facility. This is the only point of the day thus far I feel like chuckling … Yeah, I'd like to bring in medicine that will make me forget about the next ten days. Got a drug for that? Let's see… I have a fear of crowds, enclosed spaces, heights… Is it too late for my therapist to write me a note to get me out of here? I highly doubt any of these excuses carry enough weight to help me break free of the grasp of the penal system. I hesitantly write "none" in each space and sign off.

As I'm handing back my medical release, I overhear a conversation between one of the ladies and the intake guard.

A sixty-seven–year-old woman, sentenced for thirty-five days (read that again, please) has admitted to having high blood pressure. They took her blood pressure and told her that if it was high, she would have to leave. Damn … Why can't I have high blood pressure? Just once I'd like to have something bad happen to me that worked in my favor. Once all our pictures are taken and IDs created, we are escorted to another smaller cell. This time we are locked in. The deafening sound of the door sealing behind me produces a simultaneous tremor throughout my body. That feeling passes as abruptly as it came, and I realize that my mind has transformed the closing click of the door into a symbolic slam. Society's anger at what I now represent is made clear by the mood and atmosphere surrounding me.

I'm looking around … metal benches along two walls and a stainless toilet and water fountain in the corner of the room. Just how long will we be here? We spend the next two hours in that room, getting to know each other, not by words—though there is some idle, softly-spoken chat—but by glances and stares. No one really makes eye contact. I'm getting a feeling that the more anonymous you keep yourself, the more tolerable this event will be. Yes, this will be my mantra for the next ten days: keep to myself and maybe no one will notice I'm here.

* * *

November 8, 2009: The Arrest

Shit … Shit, shit, shit! Why is he behind me? Where did he pull out from? What did I do? I know my speed wasn't enough to be bothered with—the cruise control was set seven miles an hour over the speed limit. Nervous Nelly that I am, I begin to quiver a little as I pull over into a parking lot off of Shea. I've been pulled over before and have always seemed to get it together enough to talk my way out of a ticket and into a warning. But then again, in previous situations I knew what I had done wrong and didn't have traces of alcohol on my breath. During the standard delay, while the officer calls in my license and does his quick investigative work, I gather my license, registration and insurance so that I can smoothly hand it over and appear cooperative. With my window already open and seat belt still on, I watch as he approaches my truck and, without him asking, hand over my documents. So begins the nightmare.

"Step out of the truck, ma'am," he sternly directs, observing me intently during the process. "Have you had anything to drink today, ma'am?" Only remembering that being cooperative in the past has worked wonders with these men in uniform, I say yes.

"How much have you had to drink?"

"A few beers." Fuck. I now know where he's headed with this and there's no possible way to get him to focus on anything else.

A couple more questions: "Where were you coming from? Do you know why I pulled you over this afternoon?"

My cooperative answers evoke no reaction from him as he tells me that he has been following me since Fountain Hills. Apparently I swerved out of my lane more than once. Okay. I think I can explain this away so that he'll just let me off with a stern warning about multi-tasking while driving. "I'm sorry, officer. I must have been looking down while putting CDs into my player."

He directs me back into my vehicle and takes my license,

insurance card, and registration back to his car while I wait for his next move. Even though the questions about what I've had to drink have me a little shaken, I still feel pretty confident that I've successfully turned this police stop into a small enough burden not to earn me a ticket and the subsequent mounds of paperwork I hear tickets require. I'm sure he's going to see that I have no priors and that he'll just tell me to pay more attention behind the wheel. I sit back and wait. And wait.

Quickly glancing at my rear view mirror, I see a second set of flashing lights approach and pull up behind the first patrol car. The knots in my stomach and throat cause me to momentarily hyperventilate. What the fuck … why is he here? The officer must have called for backup. No way … this can't be happening. As they approach my vehicle on either side of the truck, the original officer asks for my consent to administer a field sobriety test. Fucking great … I am certain that the only thing that will keep me from passing this test is nervousness. Still, I agree to take it.

"May we search your vehicle?"

I agree. Even though I have a "conceal & carry" license for my hand guns, I am glad I left my Sigsauer 9mm at home this trip. The backup cop opens my door and sees a front seat full of CDs, the mini cooler with an empty beer bottle, and my purse. He shuffles his hand through the stack and opens the glove box in hopes of finding something other than the routine napkin and ketchup packet. The search ends and, other than the empty beer bottle, they don't find anything of significance. In the absence of damning physical evidence against me, the sobriety field test begins. Toe to toe for nine paces. Standing on one leg. ABCs backwards. In my mind, I graduate with honors, successfully completing each. It's the next test I'm not so sure about …

"Could you please blow into the breathalyzer?"

"If I don't, I automatically lose my license for a year, right? "

"I can't answer that, ma'am."

Right. You, as an officer upholding the law, are completely oblivious to what happens if I choose to decline the breathalyzer. I'm about to lose it. After a very brief explanation of what type of blow he wants out of me (don't take that out of context, please) I go ahead and blow into the machine. I see 0.15 on the digital read-out. Without reporting to me the results, the officer tells me to turn around and put my hands behind my back. As I turn, a tow truck appears from around the corner and pulls up right in front of my truck. It's now obvious that the field tests were done to kill time so that the tow truck could arrive while everyone was still at the scene. The arresting officer must have made two calls when he went back to his car with my documents—one for backup and the second for a tow truck. Bastards. I wasn't even given a chance to prove my sobriety … Not that I might have qualified for a free pass … It just irritates me that I was presumed drunk before I had a chance to prove I was.

After reading my rights, he handcuffs me. As the arresting officer put me into the back of his police car—his hand on my head so I don't bump it on the door jamb—I watch my truck being loaded up onto the tow truck. Tears flowing and anger and fear mounting, I try to pull my thoughts together to determine where he's taking me. Perhaps to the station to begin the booking process.

"We're taking you to get blood drawn."

That answers that. Still trying to cooperate despite my inner hysteria, I agree to the BAC—or blood alcohol testing.

Wondering where they take DUI suspects for this procedure, I can only hope that this test will result in a different outcome. If we drive around long enough, maybe the level might drop below .08, the legal limit.

No such luck. Within minutes of loading at the scene, we pull into the parking lot of Scottsdale Healthcare, located right around the corner, and walk into the back door. As the cop unhandcuffs me, we are met by a nurse, who promptly leads me to a small room where he preps my arm for a blood sample. Hospital workers walk past and cast disapproving glances at me before continuing on. Less than ten minutes later, I'm wearing the silver bracelets again in the back of the squad car, heading to the Via Linda police substation to be processed.

Pictures are taken, fingers are printed, and I am placed in a holding cell. Four walls, a concrete floor, and a stainless steel toilet. No sink. I take a seat on the cold floor and pull my knees close into my chest, head buried between my knees. I look up and around, but I'm not sure why. There is nothing to see. My mind is now racing through my rolodex of thoughts. Filed under the "I'm really fucked" section, each one is more miserable than the next. An officer opens the holding cell and leads me out into a small room. The table is littered with the contents of my purse.

"What medications are you carrying?" he asks, his voice accusatory.

"Migraine pills and aspirin."

"We're going to have to dispose of them, since they are not in their original packaging."

Whatever. I just want to get this over with. He takes all my stuff, shoves it back into my purse, and walks out with it, saying, "We're still waiting for the paperwork to be processed.

I'll be back with your paperwork once it's complete."

I don't say a thing. After keeping me waiting for another twenty minutes, the officer escorts me to the counter to retrieve my belongings and paperwork. Strangely enough, they slide all my things over to me, handing me my money from my wallet separately. You guys went through my wallet and pulled out my cash? What on earth for? Disgusted, I look across the counter and ask for my house key.

"Ma'am, we don't have your house key."

"It was on my key chain when you took it from me."

"Then it's with your vehicle at the tow yard. Sorry."

"How do you expect me to get home and into my house?"

She shrugs her shoulders and says, "We have a cab outside waiting for you."

To state the obvious, this is a huge problem. No way to get the house key and no sympathetic ears to be found. I guess I'll have to break in to my house and hope I don't get arrested for B&E. I go outside, get into the cab, give the driver my address, and off we go. My Middle Eastern cabbie says nothing to me, but I understand why. It's difficult to carry on two conversations, one on his cell phone in some Arabic language and another one in English with a customer in the back of his cab. Doesn't matter anyway. The silent cab ride gives me a moment away from the chaos to mentally process what has taken place in the last few hours. All I know is, this is just the beginning of long rocky uphill road, and I'm walking barefoot.

CHAPTER 4

It's 9 a.m. Some male prisoners in pink stripes (Sheriff Joe Arpaio's signature clothing line) have arrived and are delivering breakfast—a gourmet selection of bread, peanut butter, cookies and an orange. I eat the orange and decide to save the bread and cookie for later in the day. Another hour passes, with zero to do except eavesdrop on stories and look at my watch. The door unlocks. I look down at my watch—10 a.m.—and I hear my name called.

Finally … I can get out of this hole and … wait … what am I thinking? …They're not moving me into a hotel room with clean towels and a private bathroom. No, my next stop won't be any better. In fact, I should assume the worst.

And now, as I look around, I can see I was right. Only this time I'm alone in the cell. Not knowing how long these new gray walls will surround me, I sit and wait. I look down at the cookie in my hand and take a bite. Wow … what bakery can stay in business making cookies this horrible? I eat it regardless. Unable to fight the urge to sleep, my body tells me it's shutting down. I think it's safe to take a nap. It's not like I'm going to miss anything. If they want me, they can just come in and wake me, if I don't wake on my own.

Surprisingly, I am able to sleep a whole hour. As I check my watch, a guard opens the door and barks an order: "Step out of the cell and put your hands together in front of you." Before me are several men in street clothes connected with a pink handcuff chain (another signature Arpaio accessory) and standing outside another cell. It appears they've stopped briefly while another convict is added to the chained lineup. They shuffle along in pairs with their ankles and wrists in cuffs, all shackled together. The guard cuffs me and, while he doesn't attach me to the chain gang, I'm ordered to follow behind, the only woman in the entire group.

Feeling as if we have walked about two blocks, we arrive at a black van. No windows in the back and I'm pretty certain there's no A/C inside the holding section. The shackled men are loaded through the side door, which is then slammed closed. Only two of us are left. We walk around to the back of the van, where there are two separate seating areas. The unmistakable odor of man-smell pours out of the opened doors as we each load into our own section. Once again, the doors are slammed closed. Pitch dark. If it weren't for the separating wall in the back, my knees would be touching those of my fellow solo passenger. Crew cut, Hispanic, and draped in stripes, he appears to be headed to where they keep the more violent criminals. Only a small section on each wall is grated for air circulation … or maybe the grate is there so everyone can enjoy idle conversation on their way to jail … you know, talk about their kids, exchange phone numbers, meet up for a cup of coffee on the outside … Somehow I doubt it, though. No one speaks. This is all very creepy. How did I go from taking my dogs on daily morning bunny chases around the neighborhood to being handcuffed and thrown in jail? My eyes well up as I try to hold back the tears.

The van parks and we all get out, walking single file. About ten minutes later, the "yard" appears. The guards separate me from the men, and now I'm left standing alone in an outside area ... After fifteen minutes, a female guard comes and tells me to strip down to one layer of clothing, remove my shoes, and put my hands up over my head along the chain link fence. Spread-eagled against the fence, I am searched and patted down. Pretty thorough search. She now knows what the contour of my inner thighs feels like. A couple of calf squeezes and armpit rubs later, we walk together (with that much caressing, maybe we're dating now, according to the prison's unwritten bylaws) to "the office," which consists of a glass window with a sign on it that says, "Do Not Knock." I try to make myself invisible as I wait.

After twenty minutes, the guard opens the glass window and I hand her my ID. She writes some numbers on the card and hands it back to me. Without so much as an explanation of the 7011 now written in black marker, she hands me two rolled up blankets, a toothbrush, and toothpaste. "Walk around the building, down the hill. Your tent is on the far right." So this is it—I'm officially entering the confines that will be my nighttime address for the next ten evenings.

* * *

November 8, 2009: After the Arrest

Crying all the way home, I obsess over how this arrest is going to affect every aspect of my life. I'm really fucked now. What if work finds out ... what's my family going to think? How will I get around if I lose my license ... how much is this going to cost? The constant, panicky noise in my head is truly deafening. I have to find a way to remove the pain and emotional distress that's consuming my every thought and may well do so for the rest of my life. My only option is to permanently check out.

It's not the first time that I have contemplated ending my life. I attempted this "stunt" before, several months prior, when I was going through my breakup. I was completely devastated and didn't know how to move on. On this occasion I chose carbon monoxide asphyxiation, a fancy way of saying "taking the gas pipe." Sitting inside my running truck with the garage closed, I drank a bottle of wine and listened to some amazing music. I cried. I prayed. I really thought that this would be the end of all of the pain … peaceful sleep awaited me now. But it didn't quite turn out that way. I woke up several hours later, freezing in the front seat of my truck. Strangely enough, the ignition was turned off and I was alive and surprisingly alert, with only a small headache from the wine to show for my efforts. The ignition switch is still a mystery to me.

This life hasn't been the picture-perfect, white-picket-fence version I secretly dreamt of. Over the years and with a lot of therapy, I've come to realize that perfect lives don't exist and that each and every one of us is challenged to varying degrees. Those who approach their less-than-charmed existences with anger and hostility, feeling loss of entitlement, suffer the most. Those with positive attitudes, no matter the situation, will prevail, enjoying the good things and being satisfied with their given lots. Today I have clearly forgotten those lessons it took years to learn.

This additional stress is going to plunge me even deeper into the dark hole that I've been floundering about in over the last few years. Suicide is the only way to lift this heavy burden.

I decide, then and there, to end things.

The mind works in mysterious ways. Thoughts can make total sense one moment and seem like pure and utter lunacy the next. I am certain that this is the right thing to do and consider my pending actions matter-of-factly. No hesitation or questioning. No fear.

I arrive home and head to the back of the house to climb the seven-foot tall block fence. Without stopping to consider the consequences of what I'm about to do, I set out all the paperwork—the criminal traffic ticket, processing and blood analysis consent forms—on the table (for effect, of course), and walk into my office toward my RX drawer. Perfect—I have two different prescriptions that, if mixed with enough potency, could drop a horse. Twenty Klomapin pills (prescribed, in a smaller dosage, to calm my anxiety) and twenty or so Ambien tablets should do the trick. I swallow the Ambien first, confident that these will put me to sleep before the lethal combination can kick in.

After choking down the Klomapin, my last and probably only concern is, what do I do with my dogs? It would be easier to "check out" if I didn't have their brown eyes watching my every move. They can always sense my emotions. I've been crying, and the salty tears on my face would be reason enough for them to be all over me. I can't very well write them a note and explain what I am doing, so my only choice is to put them in the bedroom—"tuck them in" with the TV on and shut the door.

I leave my bedroom to the sound of their restlessness behind the door to search out a pen and pad of paper. I'm beginning to feel the effects of the Ambien. My eyes are getting heavy, and I need to get the note written as quickly and coherently as possible. With my mind increasingly clouded, I start the note out with I'm sorry ... then I write instructions for the care of my two dogs and how my belongings should be split up amongst the family. I have a living will in the safe. The lucky one who finds the sticky note with the combination on the bathroom mirror gets to open it first and find my emergency cash—a thousand dollars. Then I grab the box of ashes that was once my beloved pooch, V. My soul mate. My guardian angel. I want her with me. I send off an email to a girlfriend, telling her I am sorry. Two text messages and I can finally rest—one to Lucky, telling him to fuck off, and another one to a girlfriend that reads, "Thanks for being such a great friend ... catch you on the other side." I take V's ashes and walk into the spare bedroom to lie down and go to sleep for the final time.

CHAPTER 5

While searching for my bunk, I wonder what it would be like if I had to be here for months or years, instead of days. My new community … like moving to a city you've never been to before, wondering how you will survive the unfamiliarity and strangers that surround you … No signposts. No directional arrows to help point the way to your tent or where to eat. Eventually you would get comfortable enough with the layout so that you could walk it in your sleep. I don't want to get that cozy with this place. Out of the corner of my eye I see a flashing neon light coming from the guard tower and look up. It reads "Vacancy." Sheriff Joe has a sense of humor.

I ask one of the ladies standing outside of one of the tents for directions, and she is kind enough, though just barely, to point and say "over there." As I continue my walk, I see "70"… okay, maybe that's what the 70 means on my ID. The number 11 must have something to do with where my bunk is located in the tent … I nervously step into the tent and see a woman from my Alcohol Awareness classes who recognizes me. It's so nice to see a familiar face! Becky had already been here for twenty-four hours, and has another fourteen days to go—her second "vacation" at The Tent in two years. We talk for a bit and then together we look for my bunk. Just as I thought, number 11, the top of the two-bunk bed arrangement. Imagine two slabs of steel welded in the four corners to four steel square rods, with a couple of cross bars that double as a ladder to the top bunk. I can either sleep on a cold steel plate of metal or hock a mattress off an unused bed. It doesn't take long to find a mattress—there are several unoccupied bunks in our tent. Becky and I grab the four-inch-thick vinyl slab of filth and place it on my bunk. It's best that I can't see my mattress—the prison's technical term for urine smelling, filthy, vinyl-covered foam—from where I'm standing, as I don't think I could actually lie down on something so disgusting if I have to stare at it first. Using both blankets, I cover the mattress in vain, hoping to inhibit the possible transmission of a communicable disease. One thing is for sure—nothing could successfully cover up the dog shelter kennel-like smell. Becky and I sit on my bunk and catch up. She didn't talk much in the classes, but became an open book the moment we sat down. She's twenty-three and working as a salon assistant while she pursues her hairdresser's certification. Her first DUI happened when she was in the grocery store parking lot. She and another shopper both backed up at the same time, rear-ending each other. She'd only had a couple drinks before she decided to run out and pick up a few things. The other lady called the police and insisted they come out and review the accident. Because it happened on private property, no tickets were issued, but, after talking to each of the drivers, the responding officer determined that Becky had alcohol on her breath. The rest is obvious. She blew a 0.09% and was arrested on the spot. The second one—and the reason she's here for fifteen days and has to serve a forty-five day house arrest—came when she was leaving a Scottsdale nightclub. Now, with her license revoked for a year, Becky emphatically tells me that she had forgotten how much this place sucked. I am immediately struck with a sense of clarity as to why second and third-time offenders cycle through this place. Plain and simple—people forget. Or, more like they choose to filter this memory out.

The bunk in order, I walk out of the tent for a look around. Seven tents on the women's side of the yard. It looks as though I'm in the largest tent, which houses forty-four inmates based on the bed count. I'm told it is also the most popular. Many of the inmates tend to gather in my tent at all hours of the day and into the night. I'm not sure how it achieved such popularity, but I hope it isn't because it serves as the community's lesbian whorehouse. My stomach just did flips at that thought. Enough with the imagery. Let's try to focus on getting through the day and night.

High noon has brought temperatures bordering on intolerable. Arizona temperatures in April can be unpredictable. In most cases, the days are quite comfortable and the evenings cool. Occasionally, like today, the temps soar higher than normal, as the arid, scorching summer rapidly approaches.

My stomach is telling me it's time to look for something to eat and drink. I spot two twenty-four-hour vending machines containing water and soda. They appear to be available for use, but who knows if there are rules for accessing them. In my debriefing this morning with Becky, I heard a rumor about the machines—that they are purportedly owned by the Arpaio family. I don't have any proof whether or not this is true, but I wouldn't be surprised. Since I received the notice of what we could bring into prison, I was always curious as to why we would need $40 inside. Unless you're in here for an extended period, this amount is excessive if all they offer is vending machine food and drink. Now I know why—it makes perfect sense. Overprice the vending machine goods as a form of additional revenue for the prison system or the vending machine owners, whoever they are. Why not? A captive audience (pardon the pun) with nothing to do tends to eat to pass the time. Why not allow them to bring the means to buy food and drink? This regulation is actually quite generous for such an establishment.

Spending a portion of your daily $40 limit at the beverage vending machine is recommended—unless you prefer to drink out of the fifty-gallon water drum that is filled throughout the day with hose water and ice. When the guards have time, that is. The drum has been empty since my arrival. The guards don't care. I refuse to donate to the coffers of the Arpaio family or the prison system, so my only choice is to drink out of the water drum. Cups aren't supplied, so you can stick your mouth under the spigot like a dog or find a water or soda bottle somehow. I would equate the water bottles to cigarettes in the prison movies—they are a valuable commodity and can only be acquired through barter. After several minutes of searching for something to drink from, I am handed empty soda bottles by each of my two new friends and bunkmates, Melissa and Becky. I hope there's no expectation of payback; I haven't learned the prison's bartering system yet and am not sure I want to participate. My thirst is becoming more pressing—I have to face the fact that I will have to drink from the water drum to stay hydrated. I head toward one of the guards to let him know that the drum is empty. "Could we get the water drum filled please?" Without a word, he hands me a three-foot hose and a tool to turn on the hose water; he is apparently too busy to do his job. Mission accomplished, sort of. So here I stand, filling the drum as if it were for a pasture of farm animals. Maybe I'll spread some hay around during feeding time.

"Did the guards give you ice to put in the drum?" one of the girls asks me.

"No." She turns and walks toward the guard, who is about fifteen feet away.

"Sir, excuse me, but is there any way we can get ice for the water drum?" she requests in a very respectful way.

"Too busy. Sorry. Maybe tomorrow." The guard answers sarcastically as he stands there motionless, arms folded, as if conserving energy for his trip home. The brief glance she gives him as she walks away is priceless. I have a feeling that the continuous friction between inmates and guards often results in this type of interaction. I'm sure I'll be sending my fair share of angry glances as my time here stretches out. As I fill the water drum, the three women I shared the intake process with arrive. No rhyme or reason to the processing time. It can take anywhere from twelve to eighteen hours for inmates to complete the intake process. We acknowledge each other as I keep the hose in the barrel. Before I can finish filling it, the women begin to line up to fill their bottles. I get in a line of about five women, waiting my turn to drink hose water from a plastic barrel. One day you're ordering a Silver Oak cabernet from a swanky restaurant, the next … well, you get the picture. Still, I step up to the barrel during my turn, fill the bottle, and drink the entire thing. What have I just done? The aftertaste and smell literally make me ill. A nearly lethal combination of rust, minerals, and shit is apparently on tap today. Now I know what my friend's dog is expecting as she makes her way to my toilet to get a drink.

I speed walk to the bathroom, thinking that if I'm going to get sick, at least I have the decency to find a toilet. As I walk in, a small dry heave stops me dead in my tracks. The unsanitary conditions just about make me toss my cookies … literally. Maybe that's how the phrase "toss my cookies" got started. An inmate, forced to eat the prison food cookies, heads to the bathroom to give them back … Eight filthy sinks, with the same number of open stall toilets, several of which are unflushed or plugged. C'mon people … it's already disgusting in every other corner of this place … should we really suddenly ignore the post-defecation flush reflex to add to the stench? Prison movies are spot on when they depict open, high school style shower quarters off of the bathroom. If you can stand the smell and are comfortable being spotted naked by a toilet user, then the shower area is for you. A couple of dry heaves and I begin to feel a bit better. I have learned my lesson—sip the hose water or it will find its way back out. By 8 p.m. the drum is empty.

* * *

More Fallout from the Arrest

It's clear now that this has become an in-body experience, not the intended out-of-body event I imagined. I'm surprised that my arms and legs are not strapped to the bed … the only restraints I can see are the clear tubing that connects my hand with the drip feeder and the wires that connect the heart monitor patches attached to both sides of my upper chest. Waking up to visions of friends and family in the ICU is both troublesome and comforting. With failure comes accountability and now, with all the other crap that was supposed to follow me to my resting place, I have to deal with the family inquisition and blame for my actions. I admit, though, that having family around me, no matter how harsh their judgment, is reassuring. In the past, my "reaching out" phone calls only resulted in excuses as to why everyone was too busy to help. I just needed a stage to vent my life's struggles to anyone who had a vested interest in listening. I guess a hospital bed and an attempted suicide—stage and storyline—have brought the interested parties together.

So here they are. Sitting around, chatting amongst themselves, walking in and out of the hospital room … like detectives, waiting for me to gain consciousness so they can find answers that will justify their presence. The race between those who feel guilty and those who have wiped themselves clean of any responsibility is too close to call. Split about fifty-fifty. "What could I have done to prevent this?" has given way to "She's a big girl and needs professional help." Never mind that I've been seeing a therapist fairly steadily for the past eight years. Regardless of their opinions, their concern for me will fade fast—in all likelihood, the moment they step out of the hospital.

It's all a bit much to bear. Who found me? How could I still be alive after that massive overdose? I lie purposefully motionless, even though I can faintly hear the conversation around me, so that no one will notice I'm coming around. Maybe they'll just give up hope that I will wake … I need them all to leave soon, so I can finish what I started.

Finally. Alone in the room. I spot a meal tray on the table and a plastic knife. With my free right hand and a twisting lean, I manage, in my weakened state, to reach over and grab the knife. I don't have much time—the nurses are in and out of these ICU wards fairly often. It's like trying to saw wood with a butter knife, but I manage to break the skin of my left wrist and now have a pretty decent stream of blood running down both sides of my hand. The sedatives have deadened the pain, so all I really feel is a little burning and the warmth of the blood. A more strategic plan would have likely given me a better shot at success, but thinking clearly is not on my résumé these days.

Damn it ... The nurse is back and not too happy to find bloodied sheets and a patient hell-bent on removing her hands at the wrist ... I'm sure it won't take long for her to call in the suicide watch team. Is there such a thing? Prisoners and detainees who are considered high risk for suicide attempts are closely monitored by someone or something. Maybe they have this program in hospitals as well. All I know is that I'm zero for two ... no three... I somehow had forgotten that several months back, when I was going through my breakup with Lucky, I decided to look for eternal peace via carbon monoxide. That attempt still bewilders me to this day. I've read somewhere that failed suicide attempts are more the result of needing attention than wanting to die. It's difficult for me to say if, in my case, I was in dire need of attention or if I truly wanted to end the mental anguish I was feeling. If the actions following this attempt are any indication, my guess is that I was reaching out for help. I got out of the truck, went inside, and called my therapist. Between the two of us, we spent the next several months dissecting the suicide attempt and how to use the experience in some life-enriching way.

Now, by virtue of my ineptitude, I have raised the red flag to the staff here. I will need to be monitored 24/7. Sedated now, my eyelids get heavy as I begin to doze off ...Waking to early morning commotion, I witness two female nurses and a man in blue scrubs, definitely not a doctor, begin to prep me for a change of scenery. Must need the ICU room for some other lost soul who's run into bad luck. One nurse untangles the tubes leading to my backhand and frees up the wheels on my drip system, preparing it for motion. The other nurse collects all of my personal belongings and places them on the bed next to me as I sit up. I stare at the male nurse's balding head as he holds the wheelchair steady. His firm grasp of my elbow as he helps me move from the bed into the chair is strangely comforting. With my things on my lap, I'm wheeled out of ICU … None of them say much … I hear a few mumbles that could be enlightening, except I'm too groggy to put them together in my head to form any semblance of a sentence. I'm sure they know what they're doing.

An elevator ride later, I arrive at the entrance to a regular hospital room, and, luckily for me, no roommate … at least for the moment. I'm feeling a bit more alert than when I left the ICU—enough to remind myself that reality has set in: I am in an even bigger mess than before.

No more faking sleep with the relatives around. The sedatives have been eliminated from my hourly diet and now it is time to face family scrutiny. I didn't really process anything other than their presence in the ICU, so it will be another new experience to see their reactions to my situation. It won't be long now …

The doctor on call hastily walks in and goes right to my chart to check my vitals. Too embarrassed to strike up a conversation, I just lie there trying not to make any sudden moves that would alert him that I am conscious. Too late. "How are you feeling?" he asks without so much as glancing up from the chart.

"I'm fine, all things considered," I answer, forcing the

words out with a dispirited sigh.

"The nurses will take good care of you on this floor. Let them know if you need anything."

Gee, thanks doc. That was revealing. The ICU nurses won't let me die and my guess is that the suicide watchdogs won't let me leave. He quickly scampers out of the room and I decide to rest up for the inevitable.

My next visitor wakes me from an early stage-one REM state. "Hi, I'm Doctor Kasey and just want to talk to you for a short moment." His clipboard hides his notes as he begins to ask me questions. I can barely understand him—I'm not even awake. If I just give him a few short one or two word answers, maybe he'll leave and I can get some rest. It works. He doesn't stay very long and now I can get back to some shut-eye. After he's been gone for less than a minute, I can't remember the questions he asked. No big deal—I'm sure it's just routine stuff meant to fill in a few blanks on the chart.

Damn it. Why is everyone making all this noise? Can't this unstable mind get some rest? The commotion this time is from my mother, brother and sister. With tears in their eyes, they each assume a unique expression, paralleling their attitude toward me. Mom looks worried and guilty. Sister looks disapproving and judgmental, and brother smirks, as if to say, "Way to go, champ … What are you going to do for an encore?" They are grateful that I'm alive, which I interpret to mean that they acknowledge I exist.

"Don't ever do this again!" sister blurts out as if *this* means everything I've done that she's ever disapproved of leading up to this hospital stay. She has no basis for judging my drug or alcohol dependency. She buried herself in eighty thousand dollars of gambling debt in just a couple of years. Hypocrite.

Each in turn begs me not to try this again. They seem genuinely concerned ... concerned by this interruption in their daily routine. Too rough on them, I guess. I'm sure it's a huge inconvenience to make an extended appearance at the hospital, but it is necessary in order to confirm their love and concern for the benefit of the hospital staff and fellow family members. Their collaborative question of 'why' isn't even posed; they either know the answer or are not prepared for it. Obviously they have not been listening to me over the past year.

I carry the main burden for this lack of communication. I'm certainly not one to open up and spill my emotions to those who traditionally lack empathy. Pain and loneliness are cryptic feelings meant to be understood only by those who are faithful followers of my life story.

"Rita and her husband found you on the bed of your spare bedroom," Mom helplessly blabs, as though breaking the promise to keep a secret. She decides to share the rest of the story.

Fuck. Why did I text Rita with the obvious, 'I'm about to kill myself, have a nice life' tone? Evidently she and Tom drove thirty minutes after receiving the message to come and check on me. While on the phone with Lucky, they found me motionless and were unable to wake me up. Rita immediately dialed her sister, a nurse in Oklahoma, to ask what to do. After calling my mother, she and Tom walked me around the house, hoping I'd wake up enough to get sick and throw up all the pills. Apparently I'd had a moment of clarity and as we walked through the kitchen ... I opened the refrigerator and grabbed a Coors Light. Talk about an embarrassing suicidal moment. Mom showed up shortly thereafter. Another moment of clarity struck with the realization that my plan had failed. In front of Mom, I grabbed a handful of pills and threw them in my mouth. Another foiled plan; Mom dug them out with her hand and quickly escorted me out of the house and into her car—hospital bound. No resistance. The drugs that had made it into my system and my suppressed desire for attention led to my being easily escorted out and poured into Mom's car.

Mystery solved.

Eager to get on with their day, sister and brother say their goodbyes and promise another visit tomorrow. Mom stays, and we both sit in the room, making small talk.

My father and stepmother arrive. This would normally be an awkward gathering, but Mom and Dad temporarily suppress their distaste for each other. Mom retreats to the background while Dad and his wife approach the bed. Experience dictates that this already awkward encounter will escalate. Dad will make promises he can't keep and his wife inevitably will find her foot firmly implanted in her mouth the moment she opens it.

Surprise! History won't be rewritten today. Not thirty seconds into the conversation, my step-monster decides it's the perfect moment to tell me she thinks I have a drinking problem. Skips right over the 'how are you feeling' question and goes straight for the kill shot.

I ignore her like I always do. No need to reward this sort of behavior with a response. Whether or not I have a problem with alcohol is for me to discuss with my counselors and therapists—not with family looking for a quick and easy diagnosis and explanation for my actions. Equating DUI with alcoholism is a common correlation made by those who have never been arrested for a DUI. However, to paint with such a broad, ignorant stroke is unfair. I know that they have all operated vehicles over the Arizona legal limit, where an arrest is warranted if the officers determine impairment to the slightest degree.

My dad, after a quick side bar with his wife right before sending her off on a coffee hunt, finds himself alone with me and eager yet hesitant to say something meaningful. I think he's trying to find the right words—not easy for him—and certainly uninspired by his wife's example. Guilt has a way of surfacing statements that ring hollow, and his apologies are no exception.

"I know that I haven't been around when you needed me … I can only say that I'm sorry for that … We need to spend more time together and to make that happen." Blah, blah, blah.

Sure, Dad. How about next week we grab dinner? I would bet the whole cost of this DUI on his no-show or cancellation if we were to schedule a date. I won't bother to set one. I haven't seen or talked to him in three months and he hasn't initiated contact in over a year. I'm sure he has his hands full with my step-monster. I explain that I'm tired and really just want to sleep—but thank him for coming.

As history dictates, family pops into my life only when they are in need. This time they are in need of reassurance that no one in their ranks falls outside their definition of normal. It's rare that any of them dig deeper into my spirit for the sole purpose of getting clarity on what floats my boat. I don't blame them. Focus on their immediate families certainly should come first. The last thing I want is for them to shine the spotlight squarely on me. Givers are uncomfortable with being the center of attention. But here I am, squarely on the radar screen, blinking like a smoke detector in a dark room. I'm a mental mess and now it's time to figure out how to limit the family's impact on my state of mind and take my life back.

The rest of my second evening in the hospital consists of long naps, with brief nurse visits to check vitals and offer food and water. Tomorrow I should be able to walk out of here, pull things back into focus and get back on track.

The hospital does not take suicide attempts lightly. When I ask the nurse about leaving, she says that by law I have to be monitored for thirty-six hours before being released. Who knows when that clock started ticking. I've been here for … let's see… thirty-four hours now, which in my opinion has covered most of the mandatory time period. Figuring that I will hit my first thirty-six hours by 10 a.m., I begin pushing for a check-out time. I hit the nurse call button and wait. Even though I am fully awake and ready to go home, getting the attention of a nurse proves more difficult than when I was sedated. After several minutes have passed, a male nurse comes in. "When can I get out of here?" I ask in my sane voice.

"Sit tight. We're waiting for a bed to open up."

What does that mean? Only a couple of seconds pass before I start shaking, as I realize the implications of his statement. Plans are in motion to send me to a psychiatric hospital. I cannot bear the thought of being sent off to some asylum. They can't take me there against my will. I'll refuse. How can they arbitrarily send me off like this? Forty-five minutes pass and I get angrier at the sudden lack of attention from all of the medical personnel. A doctor I don't recognize appears from around the room's corner entry.

"Good morning. How are you feeling?"

"Fine …" I say, angrily over-articulating each letter. "When can I leave?"

"We're working on opening up a room for you at Banner Behavioral Health Hospital, so it will likely be this afternoon."

"Well, there's no WAY I'm going anywhere but home … and whoever approved this psych hospital for me never bothered to get my permission … What's your name?"

"I'm Dr. Kasey. During our discussion yesterday, it seemed that you were open to this move."

"I hardly remember speaking to you yesterday and I certainly don't recognize you. You made a decision based on an interview I gave you while I was drugged up? That doesn't seem right."

"Let's start over. If you feel strongly about going home, we are going to have to lay down some ground rules."

Dr. Kasey details our conversation from yesterday. Needing to influence anyone who has the power and authority to ship me off to a mental facility, I interview with a doctor who works for social services. An interview with another staff psychologist at the hospital is enough to convince them I am okay to go home, with three conditions: (1) I am to be released to my mother's care and watchful eye, (2) I will immediately follow up with treatment at an out-patient treatment facility of their choice, and (3) I have all my guns removed from my house.

Fine. Agreed. If that's what it's going to take to get home and begin my passage through this mess, then so be it.

Mom and Sister arrive and, as I'm wheeled out of the hospital, I glance down at my new wrist tattoo and realize I've got a long road back to stabilization. The scar will serve as a good reminder of how I got to this point, but will be a tough one to explain to anyone who notices.

The knowledge that I am returning home is soothing, yet I feel anxiety due to the circumstances surrounding the last time I was here. Secretly I wish for Mom and Sis to stick around for a while as we pull up. I'm not exactly sure how I will react as I step back in. Without having to be asked, they both get out of the car and follow me in.

The dogs are happy to see me—comforting that they don't know or care about the last few days … they still get excited and parade around now that 'Mom's' back. I feel as if I've returned home after working on the road for a few days. I drop my things off on the kitchen table and begin to cautiously scan each room for any remnants of the attempt. Looks like the notes are gone and the police paperwork has been neatly stacked on my desk. I check on my outdoor plants—dry, but alive—which coincidentally also refers to my status as I sort through this mess.

Though I didn't discuss it with her, Mom planned on staying at my house for a couple of days. She says it's easier than commuting back and forth from her small condo. What's the difference, I think; I'm paying for both places anyway. Once I'm home, calls start pouring in. Everyone wants to know how I'm doing and if they can do anything for me. I'm an expert at screening calls and today I choose to ignore them all. Surprise, surprise—a voice message left by my step-mother expresses her displeasure about my release, as if she has a say in this matter. She wants me in treatment and now I have an idea of who tried to move me from one sick bed to another. Fuck her and fuck them all. I know, shitty attitude, but where were they when I really needed them?

They don't waste any time. A call from the Crisis Prevention office lets me know that I'll be receiving a visit from an evaluation specialist within the next half hour. I'm about to start going through the motions of session therapy and doctor appointments as part of my hospital release program. No big deal, I guess. Might as well get started.

She arrives, and we say our hellos and jump right into the questions at the dining room table. I give her just enough information so that I can spare myself the embarrassment of sharing too much of my past. After some note-taking and a few phone calls, she writes down instructions of who I am to see, how many sessions, and for how long.

"I have the perfect counselor for you!" she says, brimming with confidence.

"Really. That's great," I say. I want to roll my eyes as I play along.

"This psychiatric nurse is incredible. She gets right down to the heart of the matter and has had great reviews from past patients."

Super duper. One more therapist to plug into my iPhone. I'm going to have to create a new category of therapists to go along with depression, anxiety, and pain. Who am I to argue? If it means keeping me out of the psychiatric ward, when can we get started? I escort her to the door, thank her for coming by, and make an appointment for my first visit.

I'm able to get in to see Shannon, my newest therapist, tomorrow morning. Judging from my experience in psychiatric assessment, this will proceed like all the rest. Talk about family, relationships, work, and attempts to get to the heart of how my emotions drive my actions. Getting back to my routine, I take the dogs on their daily walk and aim for an early bedtime. Tomorrow begins a new chapter.

CHAPTER 6

I decide to help the newbies get situated. It will be interesting to hear their stories; they were in the intake process for a really long time. I walk back to find both of them as clueless as I was. Janet, a widowed mother of four, and Emma, a timid introvert, are both in for DUIs as well. Emma is noticeably afraid. She explains that she had no option but to leave her four-year-old son with her unemployed boyfriend. The relationship is fairly new and she's not confident of his child-rearing capabilities. I silently wonder why she didn't bother to consider the consequences as she stepped foot in her car after a night of drinking. Who am I to wonder this? I know exactly why she didn't give it any consideration. No one does until after they are caught.

As I help them get settled in tent 70, I recognize, from the multitude of stress-related ailments I've endured in the past, that Emma is having a panic attack. She's hypoglycemic, starving, and needs food. "Chow" doesn't open until 6 p.m., so I give her my bread and peanut butter that I had stashed away for a rainy day. Most people hide money under their mattress for the proverbial rainy day ... my stash, while certainly not under my mattress, includes bread and peanut butter. Emma's reaction to deprivation has me rethinking my decision to boycott the vending machines. As much as I hate the thought of financially supporting the prison system, I don't want to end up hungry during the day, searching or bartering for a bag of chips.

Before settling in for my first night, I head back to the restroom one last time. It's now 10 p.m. and, as the guard comes around for a head check, I finally receive the remaining two blankets that were supposed to be included at check-in. I roll one of them into a makeshift pillow, and the other I unfold, place at the end of the bed, and pull over me. By evening the turtleneck from my daytime clothing ensemble (black tights, jeans, and a sweatshirt) has become a scarf to cover my face and neck.

Tonight I will manage, but tomorrow is a new day and potentially a whole new mindset. One day at a time.

* * *

My First Appointment Post-Arrest

Lucky picks me up and we head to my first appointment. Looking back, I wish I had chosen anybody else but him. I should have asked my newfound Native American friend for his phone number; he would have made a much better companion. It should come as no shock that my family decided that Lucky—my devious, workaholic ex—would be the best candidate for the job, allowing each member to bow out gracefully from the responsibility. They don't know what I know and think that Lucky is a stable, though slightly misguided, gentleman.

We hardly say two words to each other in the waiting

room. I suppose I'll have to thank him for bringing me here, but bitterness has silenced my tongue. I'm glad he doesn't get up when the nurse calls me in; I don't know what I would say if he tried to follow me. My life is no longer his business and I need to keep it that way.

I immediately click with Shannon, my new therapist. The good ones always seem to have a way to channel the internal hostility and embarrassment into something refreshingly positive. They don't try to hide behind the professional exterior and let you know right away that they realize that these situations happen to the most stable of people. In no uncertain terms, I tell her my life "is fucked." Trained professional that she is, she takes my words and reroutes my course, pointing my rickety ship northward. Her first words of advice are that I should not retain an attorney. One of her friends is an attorney for a big ambulance chasing firm in the valley and has been told over and over again that first time DUI offenders usually fare better representing themselves or getting a public defender. Not to mention the savings in legal fees. We spend several hours exchanging stories, laughing, and building a strong bond of trust. For the first time in a long while, I feel that my life is finally starting to make sense. Thank you, Shannon.

CHAPTER 7

DAY 1: Even though I've survived my first overnight, I feel as if I'm walking barefoot uphill on a rocky road; each unstable step hurts and I cannot see the road's end. Upon waking, I look around to see ten beds open. The sun is up now and the sides of the tents have been rolled up; they are quite similar to the tents in M*A*S*H; in fact, I've been told that the tents date back to the Korean War and were donated by the government. I can see into everyone else's quarters. Not that there's much to see. Women of all ages and races with no place to go. Pigeons are everywhere, positioning themselves at the top of the tent on the light fixtures. Pigeon shit covers the tops of the tents. About a dozen of them are perched right now on my tent, just hanging around. Feeding them is not allowed; signs are posted that if we feed the pigeons we could get "rolled up," meaning put into stripes and have work release taken away. The guards allow us to walk around, hang out in other tents, read, nap, and play cards—available for purchase in a vending machine in the commissary. It's all about killing time. Some of the girls roll up their shorts and sleeves and sunbathe. Another hot day, and it's only 8 a.m. The canvas tents retain heat; yesterday it reached 108 degrees, according to my bunkmate's clock/thermometer combo, and today it probably will continue to hover around that number. I suppose I should be thankful that I didn't have to serve time in July or August. There are a lot of things I should be thankful for; I'm just not currently in a mental state where I'm prepared to thank anyone or anything.

I am out-of-my-mind hungry right now, and commissary doesn't open until the guards say it's open. At least for the women, this is the rule. No set times, but you can count on it being open twice a day. Today it opens around 9 a.m., about an hour after I have gnawed my arm off. Or at least contemplated it. "Commissary," by definition, is a supermarket for military personnel and their dependents, usually located on a military installation, but ours is missing the supermarket feel and the family trip to the base store. It consists of three vending machines, one containing toiletries such as shampoo, Chapstick and Advil. Our commissary is generally devoid of food because the men, who outnumber the women three to one, have free access 24/7. When the machines still contain chips and candy, the women at the front of the line buy it all and stash it away for later. Luck plays a huge role in whether or not you eat during commissary time.

I break my vow this morning. I guess I'm not strong after all, but I'm left no choice after serving my first overnight stay in The Tent. I snag a Lunchable, which consists of crackers, small slices of meat, and slices of cheese. I take my consolation prize back to my bunk and open it. I didn't expect freshness so I'm not disappointed by the stale crackers, slimy meat pieces, and petrified cheese. The machines are out of candy bars and tuna—tuna … can you believe they serve tuna in an outdoor, climate-UNcontrolled environment? You're begging for some sort of toxic poisoning or, best case scenario, flu-like symptoms. Now that I've finished my breakfast, boredom awaits … what to do ….

* * *

Should I Hire an Attorney?

Of course I wouldn't be where I am today if I'd elected to heed all of the prudent advice thrown in my direction. I partially blame my vulnerable state of mind, but when I think about the fact that I let Lucky influence my decision about consulting with an attorney, I get really angry. After my enlightening session with Shannon, Lucky and I leave the office. On the way to the car, he somehow convinces me that the appointment he set up with an attorney is a good thing. "He comes highly recommended."

"I don't have the money to pay some attorney a ridiculous amount to keep me out of jail," I explain, waiting for him to agree.

"Don't worry about it … I will get the money and it will all work out…" Famous last words from the master of disguise. We head straight to the attorney's office before I can let the idea sink in.

My initial impression of the attorney and his dress code nourishes my belief that I am making a huge mistake. His drab, clumsy outfit is straight out of the seventies, but he is clearly no Perry Mason. His office reeks of lost cases and disappointed clients. I even think he's cross-eyed, probably from having to read and respond to all of the complaints sent to the bar association by dissatisfied clients.

He launches into the typical sales pitch one would expect to hear for a DUI case—he can probably get the charges reduced, prolong the process of conviction. He'll attend the hearings in lieu of my presence, handle the DMV issues ... all for a tidy sum of $5,000 with a $1,500 upfront retainer fee. Like a typical used car salesman, he spews, "Let me step out of the room so you two can think about it. I'll come back in a few minutes after you've had time to discuss your options." So let me get this straight: he can't guarantee that he can reduce the charges, he can delay the inevitable, and he will represent me at all the hearings. I must admit that the part about his representing me at hearings is attractive—my work schedule is hard to rearrange at times. This is the only advantage I can see, or better yet, understand. But $5,000 for him to be in court instead of me? I'm not seeing the value here. Lucky insists that this is the only way to go and that he'll take care of everything. I sit here, numb to the process and feeling that there are no clear alternatives.

We call the attorney back in, having decided to retain his services. "Great. I'll get the paperwork started. Give me about ten to fifteen minutes and we'll have you on your way home." The pit in my stomach has now grown to the point where it's making me nauseated. I may be a mess, but instinct tells me to follow Shannon's advice, not Lucky's. Presented with the invoice for the retainer, I do nothing, waiting for Lucky to step up and reach for his wallet. "Why don't you put it on your American Express instead, so that you can get the points? I will get you a check later."

Ahhh ... of course—should have seen that coming. He has no intention of financially participating in this mess. But we are too far into the process now to back down. I whip out my Amex, confident that I will never see a dime from him. I really don't expect him or anyone to pay for my mistakes, but his insistence on my taking this route along with his obvious unwillingness to pay for it reveal his true character.

The attorney assures me that everything will be okay. That I won't have to go to the upcoming New Year's Eve Day court-ordered pre-trial conference, and that I won't have any driving suspensions or jail time until the spring of 2010. You pay a professional for advice and services that you can hang your hat on, so I begin to redirect my attention to work— trying to make as much money as possible before my actual "day in court."

The rest of December I slip back into my same old habits—joining friends for holiday dinners, drinks, etc. I even drive a few times after having a few beers. No WAY would I get caught again ... nearly an impossible fate ... lightning never strikes twice ...

I don't tell my dirty little secrets to anyone in an effort to keep my spirits up during the upcoming holidays. Ashamed and embarrassed about what I have done, I try to not think about my fate ... at least until I can't repress the thought of it any longer.

The holidays come and go. No family gatherings. No Christmas tree. I take my therapist's advice and pretend that Christmas is just another day.

Everything is dysfunctionally back to normal.

CHAPTER 8

Mom is here. Thank God. It's not like she pulls up, gets out, and rings the doorbell. We were dismissed ten minutes ago, and I've been standing outside the door, watching as cars pull up to take the released inmates home. I'm too tired to feel embarrassed as each driver momentarily stares at me before loading.

It doesn't even feel like a weekday, much less like Monday morning. I am starving. Climbing into the front seat, I know I'm giving off a foul odor but can't help it. Mom better not say anything—I may snap. She doesn't and we leave the premises. The taste in my mouth is an extension of how I smell. I swear someone shit in my mouth right before I woke up this morning ... or, more likely, it is the distaste of that place, knowing that I have nine more evenings in that horrendous penitentiary. I finally speak up and tell her to go directly to McDonalds. Craving an Egg McMuffin and a Diet Coke, I'm guessing that nothing could satisfy my need to feel separated from The Tent. Still, I am hungry, and the fact that the only thing I've had to eat over the last twenty-four hours is two oranges and a bottle of tainted hose water compels me to eat something quickly.

The stop is short—drive-through—and I am like a kid with a happy meal. We aren't five hundred yards from Mickey D's when my mouth begins to sputter what my mind is trying to process. Sleep-deprived, disconnected thoughts go hand in hand with bloodshot eyes and an upset stomach. Geez ... can I even make sense right now? How can I express anything sensible enough to invoke a helpful response? I keep spewing random words. Mom must think I'm an idiot. Or maybe she just feels sorry for me. I want to describe my experience ... I just don't think words can do it justice. Not right now, anyway. Am I euphoric to be out, if just for a few hours? Or am I feeling dread because I know I have to head back in another twelve hours for my next overnight? The confusion of not being able to express what you're feeling is unnerving. I take several deep breaths, finishing my breakfast and trying to focus on one thing at a time. My stomach now somewhat full, I center my attention on getting these disgusting clothes off my body. They need to be washed, and I need to take a long, hot shower.

As we stop in front of my townhome, I get out and rush to the door without waiting for my mom. Sorry, Mom. I've been sullied by these clothes for a full day and they aren't getting any cleaner hanging on my body. I head right for the washer, peeling off layers as I walk. The smell from the clothes is God-awful. Like I have been pissed and shit on and then rolled in the dirt. Naked, with my clothes going through a heavy/hot cycle, I descend into the step-down shower. I'm lucky in that I have one of those hot-water heaters that starts out hot—I need it to cleanse the body that just spent an eternity in hell. Nine more eternities left to go. Standing in the shower, spread-eagled, for almost twenty minutes, I wish that the hot water might also wash away my dread of having to return. No such luck—I step out of the shower and lurch to the toilet, vomiting at the thought of going back to that horrific place.

Mom has retired to the spare bedroom. I like to think that we could sit on the couch and chat about the experience, but she knows better. When I'm ready. I grab my PJs and dress quickly—not only because I'm shy, but because PJs provide the illusion that I just spent the morning at home. Who am I fooling? I woke up to fifty women in my tent, all in different stages of their morning ritual. Some still sleeping, some half-dressed, some hurrying to get out of there for work release. Obviously, I was one of the latter.

I get on my laptop and start typing everything I can remember. No structure—just words loosely assembled as thoughts and experiences. I've heard that when people experience a traumatic event, they block the experience out of their minds. As time passes, they unintentionally repress most, if not all, of the memories. The mind deals with trauma in peculiar ways, this being one of them. I know that my mind will discard this memory entirely and, while it sounds enticing now, I will regret it later. I need to recall this experience, as much as it pains me. Record every last detail of the tent, the yard, the inmates. I'm embarrassed and abhorred by the fact that I'm now "one of them"—with a DUI tattoo across my forehead. I stop typing after two hours, exhausted from the physical effort as much as the regurgitation of details. I begin to re-read what I've just typed and the disconnected bits and pieces of the first few lines are enough to plunge me into depression. Nauseated, I set the alarm for noon and take an Ambien; I need to sleep for a few hours but not so much that I find myself wide awake in the tent that evening.

Nothing works out as planned. I sleep through my alarm, waking to a 2 p.m. reading on my clock. Shit … I've got a bunch of errands to run—no way am I going to be able to knock them out in the short time left before having to report back. I race around like one possessed—not so far-fetched, considering that my family members clearly think I could use an exorcism.

I manage to get through all my errands with a little time to spare, so I call my newest friend and current bunk-mate Melissa to see if she still needs a ride. Melissa is twenty-two, single, unemployed and in college. She was convicted of an extreme DUI after she totaled her car in an accident. Her fifteen-day sentence began a day before mine and, since her license is suspended and she no longer has a car, she's hard-pressed to find an inexpensive way back and forth for the next two weeks. We make plans for the evening. These aren't typical "let's go grab a drink and check out what's playing" plans. Like armed forces generals, we plot, right down to the last detail, how the night is going to play out. It will start with the pre-entry meal. It can't be consumed any sooner than fifteen minutes before our arrival or we might get hungry and have to eat the crap they are serving. Finding food that will be both filling and yet limit our trips to the lavatory proves to be more challenging than anticipated. After several "what ifs," we settle on turkey wraps from a local deli. Next we discuss beverages. The strategy is to avoid caffeine before the evening sets in, but we will also need beverages after we are released in the morning. We pack my cooler full of ice to carry the wraps, water bottles, diet Dew and Dr. Pepper.

The final and probably most important decision for the evening is what to use as a sleep aid. With many choices—my medicine cabinet is full of mind-altering prescription drugs—

I pick a combination of Xanax and Ambien. Melissa decides to stick with over the counter—two Advil PMs. We say our goodbyes and I head out the door to pick her up.

* * *

First Court Date

The New Year arrives and, as expected, I really don't have a lot to look forward to. Between court dates, alcohol awareness classes, fines, and the mother of all judiciary mandates—jail time—2010 is looking like a total washout. As for resolutions, I have too many to choose from. We always want to right the ship of self-destruction through a New Year's resolution—stop smoking, lose weight, etc. I decide that mine is simply to get through the year.

Yesterday's New Year's Eve court date—the one I was required to attend but my attorney handled in my place—was a pre-trial conference, where both sides determine if the evidence warrants taking it to trial or if it will become another status quo DUI offense. Having been told not to worry, I didn't, although it would have been helpful to know what was discussed. By attending for me, my attorney allowed me to work during the holidays, a paycheck that would cover a fraction of my mounting expenses. I'm in Kansas City today and plan to fly back home this afternoon.

My truck has been sitting in my garage since I retrieved it from impound a couple of months back. While it's my one status symbol and a former source of self-esteem, it is also now a constant reminder of that fateful day and must be sold to pay off debt and free up cash. The decision to sell is painful; I bought the truck used, but it's loaded with everything I want—on-board computer for my music, leather, black on black. Owning it made me feel financially fit. With its sale, my social status shifts from upper crust to trailer trash, like having to travel on a bus after flying first class.

I remember a friend who went through a dreadful period when he was fired from his job, was going through a divorce, and had to hold a rummage sale to raise money to stay afloat. He finally landed on his feet a couple of years later, but it wasn't because of the survival sale—that money was spent on gas and a case of wine—it was because he persisted and refused to let the situation define him. As for the truck, what choice do I have? It could sit in my garage for a year, or it could help to fix my mistake. Tomorrow I'll list it on Autotrader. I'm finally making good decisions and feel as though this is one of many to come. The price I paid for the truck was higher than the market price; I hope to sell it for what I still owe.

Costs associated with this DUI to date: $8,297.61—a mind-boggling total. And there are more expenses to come. While I'm able so far to cover costs by picking up more work hours and selling off my prized possessions, others in my situation are not so lucky. Take out a loan, have Daddy pay, borrow from friends … none of these are good options. Pay or do without a valid driver's license until you can. That's possible in commuter cities like New York or Boston, but in Phoenix or L.A., where getting anywhere requires a vehicle, you are placed in a seriously compromising position.

CHAPTER 9

The next ninety days of my new life are all about work and completing a daunting list of requirements. Racking up work hours to allow for the upcoming required class time takes the top position on my to-do list. After all, the last item on this unenviable list is scheduled to start in April.

Friday, February 26, 2010: My Punishment Begins

Yesterday I was told by the clerk in the courtroom that I had to contact the facility within twenty-four hours to set up my screening and the subsequent classes. Otherwise, a warrant would be put out for my arrest. Really?? What … are you afraid I'm going ignore your request and skip town? Does everything have to make me sound so criminal? All I want to do is to get through all my punishments and suspensions as soon as possible. I don't want this to drag on and on. I hoped to not have to deal with anything after The Tent other than the interlock device for my new used truck.

As commanded, I make the call and set up the screening for today at Scottsdale Treatment Institute, which is less than two miles from my house. Perfect. Dressed in a suit for my "screening," I'm met by some recovering addict dressed in blue jeans and a baseball cap. I wonder what he might have done to work at this place and play receptionist to new class inductees. I take the paperwork he hands me and, as the door closes behind me in the empty room, begin to fill it out. After I complete the forms and take them to my counselor's office, I found out that he IS the "counselor" assigned to me. Taggart, or "Tag" for short, starts reviewing the forms with me, as if to make sure I didn't misrepresent or understate any of my answers. We briefly discuss the purpose for the alcohol awareness classes, how often I drank and where, my BAC level when pulled over, and my overall disposition in the case. I am relieved that Tag is only giving me the "minimum" hours. He tells me that I look like a respectable, upstanding person (as opposed to a falling down, jobless drunk). Thirty-six hours seems like a lot of time, but if that's the minimum, I certainly won't argue.

Classes are offered Monday through Friday, nine a.m. to twelve noon, and one to four p.m. Two Saturday classes are also offered per month, eight a.m. to four p.m., but only one of these can be counted toward the total. I have to get a couple of dates on the books before I leave his office. After I fill him in on my unusual work schedule, Tag explains to me that his office is pretty flexible if a date becomes inconvenient. I schedule my first class for Saturday, March 3rd.

The price tag: $60 a pop. Not knowing what to expect, I assume they'll be like AA meetings. Been to those in support of a friend. People gathered in the evening at some high school cafeteria or church multi-purpose room with the hope that if they surround themselves with similar addicts and their stories, they can make it through another day of sobriety. I hope this is the case. I could use one big support group to survive the next few months.

Saturday, March 3, 2010:
My First Alcohol Awareness Class

Arriving a bit earlier than the eight a.m. start time, I'm nervous, ashamed, and anxious. Being one of the first to show, I watch everyone else enter. They remind me of freshmen in high school, walking into homeroom for the very first time. Everyone is subdued as they circulate, looking for places to sit. Their timid expressions—no eye contact—add to the library-like atmosphere. To pass the time I count them— eighteen with potentially a few more stragglers in the hallway or outside finishing their smokes. The instructor enters the room a few minutes after eight, introduces himself as Dave, and passes around nametags to fill out. He doesn't look to be in a very good mood this morning, but how would I know? Maybe he's just an ornery recovering addict who is required, as part of his own court-ordered sentence, to lead these classes. In a powerfully demeaning tone, he tells us to take everything off our desks, turn off our phones, and give him our complete attention. Okay. Nothing like an AA class now.

Dave begins going around the room, starting at the front right row. He asks the first guy his name, age, and why he's here and is clearly not in the mood to hear the obvious answer: "because it's required by the court." Kevin, twenty-six, got his DUI coming back from a Cardinals game in October. He had one more friend to drop off when he was pulled over. Funny thing was, after Kevin failed the field sobriety tests, the cop took him over to have blood drawn and allowed the friend to drive his car to the station to wait for him to be booked. In my mind, common sense would dictate

MARK FEUERER

that if Kevin was driving, he was likely the most sober of the group. Perhaps not … who knows? That's all Kevin will share. After Kevin finishes his tale, Dave comments that he could have killed someone, and that it is idiots like him who decide to drive after a few drinks that provide all the headlines for the local papers.

After Dave's particularly prickly critique, Susan, next in the line of classroom chairs, isn't so forthcoming. She is fifty-three and got her DUI leaving a strip mall pub after a happy-hour work function. Dave spends the rest of the class badgering and humiliating, calling on each and every one of us to "tell him the scoop" on why we are here, always finding a way to slip in a snide remark about our behavior. Surprisingly, when he gets to me, my brief story triggers very little response; he is probably short on time and ran out mean things to say.

Finished with the introductions, Dave signals the guest speaker to come in. What a relief. His unrelenting tirade has made us all feel about three inches tall. Maybe the next guy can provide some enlightenment and education. The new guy is Ken Sharp, a radio talk show host out of Los Angeles. His hour-long show, *Ridin' Dirty Radio,* discusses drinking and driving laws. Now we're getting to some interesting material. The subject matter, which focuses on inspiring people to learn to enjoy alcohol without risking legal trouble, makes me perk up. His direct experience inside Arizona's DUI system makes what he has to say potentially motivational. But let's wait and see. After all, he's a guest in Dave's class, which means he could be just another of the Devil's minions in disguise.

As I find myself paying closer attention, Ken talks about the inhumanity of Tent City, the lack of viable public transportation in Phoenix, and how we can get involved to help change laws. Just as I'm getting into the subject matter, there is a brief pause in Ken's presentation, and Dave takes over, calling us all alcoholics: "You all deserve jail time ... and make no mistake ... you are the lowest forms of life on the planet." Very constructive, Dave. Thanks for that. He warns us that if we do not continue to participate in his class, he will kick us out, forcing us to start over. Can he actually make us take additional classes? Hell, I certainly don't want to start over. Whatever you need, Dave. Let's just get through this.

Later, while walking my dogs after a full Saturday of verbal abuse, I begin to cry. No more ... PLEASE. After everything that I have been through, someone found a way to actually make me feel worse. Tag should have warned me that the classes with Dave would be pure and utter hell. After my experience, I want to warn anyone and everyone to avoid classes that Dave is instructing. I feel as if it is my duty to bring attention to his surly and abusive nature.

CHAPTER 10

DAY 2: After I dropped Melissa off this morning, it was decided that the best time to leave her place to ensure a safe and early arrival would be 5:30 p.m. This would allow us extra time during the Phoenix rush hour.

I have been able to finish all the little chores today and now, with just a half hour left before I have to leave, I get on my computer. Emails are an afterthought today, as they will be every day until I finish my time served. No emails worthy of a response and too many junk emails to bother to scroll through. I'm killing time on the computer—not sure why. Maybe I feel the need for someone I care about to reach out to me. To feel needed, whatever the reason. Nothing today. I'll ignore the feeling of uselessness; I know it's unfounded.

What would happen if I had a beer before leaving for Melissa's? On the drive to her house, I decide I wouldn't feel any different. Would I blow over the limit? Would the guards smell it on my breath? The thought process makes the drive seem short. Melissa jumps in and we begin to review the plan. A food stop along the way—seven or eight minutes max. Drinks in the cooler. Pills in the armrest divider. So far things are going according to plan.

Arriving at 6 p.m., we have plenty of time to eat, drink, and pop the pills. Talking as she chews, Melissa begins to shed some light on her personal life. She speaks of her drinking patterns as if they are habits and mentions twice that her parents want her to move back home to keep an eye on her. She seems sincere in her desire to change. I hope she can. The DUI has inflicted some serious scars on her life financially as well as socially.

As we walk toward the gate around 6:30 p.m., a lot of the other girls are waiting at the intake door. From asking around on the first day, we find out that the guards sometimes open the gates before the 7 p.m. check-in, but other times they make you wait. No real schedule to set your watch by.

This particular evening we are ushered in about 6:45 p.m. "Strip down to one layer, remove your socks and shoes, and put all of your belongings on the table." The process of undressing in the open, even down to one layer, is so humiliating. It's like the guards get off watching us unbutton and slide off clothing. I drop my sweater, book, flashlight, and two towels on the table and wait for the next orders to be barked at me. "Line up here and face the fence … and spread 'em … legs and arms out and apart, hands against the fence." So begins the physical search and pat down. Hands up each leg, starting at the ankle. I tremble with anxiety about being touched like this. So degrading. Along my sides and then up around my lower chest, with an ever-so-slight cupping of the palms at the bottom of my B-cups. A final frisk of the head and arms, and I'm free to take my things and head to the guard window for final check in.

Even though I have trouble concentrating on anything but the guard's hands touching me in nearly inappropriate ways, I am still able to take mental notes of the process. I have a full weekend—Friday night to Monday morning—coming up and there is absolutely no way I am going to survive without a sleep aid, be it Xanax or Ambien, to knock me out. I have to find a way to sneak pills in without being caught. Now that I know generally what they do, I hope to be less anxious and more perceptive the next time. Knowing exactly how the searches are conducted is critical to hatching the perfect plan.

When we arrive at our tent an AA meeting is in full swing, so we sit in on the stories. One of my intake mates, "Grandma Mary," a sixty-seven-year-old sentenced to thirty-five days (take a moment to absorb that), spots us and, with a big smile, waves us over. The nickname works for her—she secured a few more blankets for me the first night, after one of our bunkmates had checked out. The forty-eight-hour stay is taking its toll on her. With her hair chaotic and makeup worn off, it's obvious she hasn't slept.

The AA meeting ends shortly after we show up, but we manage to catch a few stories. As expected, none of the inmates whose stories we hear have been sober for very long. Some only as long as the stretch of time they've spent in Tent City. Their incarceration is just an exclamation point to their addiction.

Before settling in for the night, rearranging the bunk is first on my short to-do list. Towels from home turn into pillows and my newest blankets cover the mattress. My original two blankets retain their purposes as top covers. An extra pair of socks made it through intake that evening, because my feet were so cold the previous night. Once everything is arranged, I walk over to talk to Melissa. She has settled in and is waiting for commissary to be announced. Likewise, her interest in the commissary sparks mine. Loaded up with sleep aids, I pull out my emergency funds—a ten dollar bill, a one dollar bill and a couple dollars worth of quarters. Having sworn I'd never give additional money to the system, I'm fighting the urge to buy. Like Pavlov's dog, when commissary is announced, I am suddenly starving. As if entranced, I walk through the gate toward the vending machines before I am verbally stopped by a male guard.

"Where do you think you are going?" he sternly asks.

"Commissary," I say as politely as I can without sharing what I am *really* thinking.

"You think you can just walk by me without asking?"

No need to answer that rhetorical question. Evidently the rules have changed since last evening. Waiting for "Simon Says," I stand with my arms crossed until permission is given to proceed. Permission granted. In a rare turn of events, the vending machines are full. Faced with this unexpected bounty, I immediately buy Doritos (seventy-five cents) and beef jerky ($1.25). Too embarrassed to be seen buying and eating from the vending machine, I inhale them in the commissary room. My resolve to avoid spending money in camp has weakened, at least temporarily. I'm not sure if I'm truly hungry or just bored and in need of stimulation to feel alive. The machines don't accept ten dollar bills, only fives and change, so I am down to my last few quarters. Why did I even bother to bring in a ten dollar bill? I must have thought there was a street vendor inside selling souvenir T-shirts. Begging the girls for change proves futile. Everyone is hoarding their quarters for future purchases. With just four quarters remaining, I buy a Snickers bar for seventy-five cents and slip it in my pocket, hoping that I can snack on it after lights out without anyone knowing.

Back at the tent, Grandma Mary is sitting on her neighbor's bunk, chatting with "Mob Mom." She is in her sixties and a convicted felon. Sentenced for nine months and already a tenant in this place for three of them, she skipped bail on her last arrest after being accused of embezzling from the Mob's escort service operation. She was caught in Oklahoma and extradited to Arizona, where she spent a couple of months in stripes before moving into our section. The mother hen of our tent and probably the most feared, she knows all the guards—who treat her with respect—and takes care of the newbies. We all visit. Mostly small talk, but at least it temporarily cures the boredom. Grandma Mary, too full from chow, had just opened a Lunchables snack, which she offers to me. I don't know what my problem is this evening, but I accept and wolf down the turkey, cheese and crackers like I haven't eaten in days. The Snickers will now be my late night dessert.

The wind is starting to kick up and the sides of the tents are flapping. The noise is distracting, especially knowing that something can be done to alleviate it. Instead of dialing the Manager on Duty (as if), three of us take the initiative and head outside to try and tie down the straps. It's much harder than we thought it would be; the yard dirt and dust is kicking up and most of the straps are frayed. We manage to secure them somewhat. Back in bed and with a full belly, I try to position myself to discreetly eat my Snickers and read a little before sleep. Not five minutes after opening the book, I feel my eyelids become twenty-five pound weights. No fighting it … my neck releases the weight of my head onto the makeshift pillow and I'm out.

A loud sound startles me and propels me to my elbows. I look around to see Grandma Mary reaching over to hand me the book that apparently fell off my chest. Clicking off the light that I inadvertently left on, I close my eyes for one more try.

Another disturbance. This time it's a one a.m. bed and ID check that drags everyone in the tent to consciousness. There's no consistency to the day or night. The routines you come to rely on at home are whisked away faster than a changing stop light. Interruptions, whether it be ID checks or bathroom runs by bunkmates, take the place of the peace and quiet found in the comforts of home. All the work release IDs, including mine, are confiscated by the guard. Being the last tent checked every night virtually guarantees a rude one or two a.m. awakening. She leaves and lockdown is lifted. Melissa and I head to the bathroom, worried that we won't be able to fall back asleep, or worse yet, that we will fall into such a deep sleep that we miss the 6:30 a.m. work release. The wind hasn't died down and the temperature has dropped into the bone-chilling category.

Are you fucking kidding me? I may have been asleep for all of fifteen minutes before another bed check wakes me. The overhead lights are switched on and a large, noisy guard walks in. Thirty seconds later she leaves, but her visit causes me anxiety. Is this going to happen all night? How will I ever hear the alarm with so little shuteye? I'm not exaggerating; another such event wakes me in the middle of the night. This time, though barely conscious, I feel an additional set of blankets being pulled over me. Ruling out the guards on duty, I conclude that it's Mob Mom. Thanks, Mob Mom—You're the best prison mom ever.

I wake to find four blankets covering me. I don't remember being cold, but I hear many of the girls talk about how cold they were and plan to wear more clothing the next night. The clock reads 6:15 a.m.—time to get up, make my bunk and throw on my shoes for the trip to the lavatory. After making sure that Melissa is up, Grandma Mary and I head up campus to brush our teeth.

On our way out of the bathroom, I check on Emma and Janet, who both had intake with me. It's Emma's first morning to get out for work release. While everyone else is preparing to leave for the day, I have spare time to kill. Throwing rocks at the pigeons that have been hanging out on the lights during the night seems like a constructive idea. They kept cooing and flapping around the tent while we were trying to sleep. I gather up my belongings just as Melissa, Grandma Mary, Emma and Janet prepare to head to the gate. As we walk together we share stories. Janet dominates the conversation today. She is forty-four years old, widowed, and has four young children. Her sentence—an extreme DUI conviction and fifteen days in The Tent—forced her to lie to her kids, who are being cared for by her mother. "Away on business" was her excuse, which is ironic because she was employed before the conviction and fired after it. Tragic.

We arrive during roll call. Because we were in earshot as they started, we aren't worried about not hearing our names. My name is called last, and I head past the one guard and into the holding room. I give the guard my bunk number and he checks me off of his list. Free to leave. Amen to that. Melissa and Grandma Mary are waiting outside the gate. I'm in no mood to stand around in a coffee klatch and talk, so I continue walking as they follow closely behind. Grandma Mary needs a ride to her car; it's on the intake side a couple of miles away. The night before, on a suspended license, she drove herself to the self-surrender site. Risky, but then again, we wouldn't be here if we didn't engage in risky behavior. While we walk to my truck, I convince her to take the bus upon her return this evening. It's a mile walk from the bus stop to the entrance, but after declining my offer for a ride, she insists that she can make it on her own. As we had hoped, the cooler of water and soda that we prepared before going in the night before has stayed cold—and is a welcome sight. The wet wipes I packed temporarily take the place of a hot shower until we can return home. I never thought a wet wipe could feel so wonderful!

After dropping Grandma Mary off at her car, Melissa and I talk the whole way to her house. We both comment on how rested we feel—surprising for the number of interruptions we put up with during the night. Maybe it's part of knowing the routine or maybe we were just so exhausted from intake that our bodies shut down each time we drifted into REM. Maybe it was the sleep aids. It just feels so good to be rested and out of jail. I'm looking forward to a long, hot shower and seeing my dogs. No daytime naps needed today. Hopefully I will be ready for sleep when I get back to the "campsite" tonight.

My change of clothes and towels are washed and ready. I will have a full belly before I check back in. I am not taking any money tonight. I don't want to be tempted.

* * *

My Second Alcohol Awareness Class

Okay, I have eight miserable hours of class under my belt. Twenty-eight more to go. With the same apprehensiveness, I enter the new classroom, but this one has only … counting … eighteen comfy chairs stretched along the perimeter of the room. I'm early again, and what I observe is similar to that of the first class, although most of the attendees are more comfortable with the process of finding a chair and settling in for the next three hours. I recognize one of the guys from my Saturday class, and we acknowledge each other as he claims the empty seat next to mine. The class soon fills up and the counselor (thankfully NOT Dave) comes in to start our "group discussion." Introducing himself, Mick shares the high and lowlights of his life in about two minutes. Ex-military, ex-addict, lots of ex-wives, and extremely well-educated. I immediately sense his über intelligence as he explains the format of the class in a very professorial way—a group discussion based on random topics either of his or the class participants' choosing. Today's topic is "Change." Opening the discussion, he shares his thoughts on the DUI system as it stands today as well as the laws. Each point he makes is painfully accurate, at least according to my experience thus far, and inspires interruptions from students in the crowd, wanting to tell their stories. Because there is ample time to bitch, he goes around the room and begins the student introductions process. We have to state our names, where we are in the "process," and what we are doing to change our lifestyles. I'm actually enjoying this class. The atmosphere is open and relaxed, so I know I'll be leaving with a much better mindset than after the first one. Everyone seems comfortable enough to open up, as comments and opinions, interlaced with strong profanity, fly around the room. Mick is fine with the strong language and even drops the F bomb himself on several occasions. After thirty minutes I feel ready to share my story. No one is here to judge, criticize or humiliate.

As the Bible states in Matthew 7:1-2,

1 Judge not, that you be not judged.

2 For with what judgment you judge, you will be judged: and with the measure you use, it will be measured back to you.

(New King James version)

This verse was recently explained to me; we should all be careful when and how we pass judgment, because there is a spiritual reciprocity that exists around us. We should examine our own motives and conduct instead of judging others. The traits that bother us most in others are usually those that are also present in us. I'm what you might call a passive believer. I believe in God and go to church on occasion, but I don't think of myself as particularly religious. I pray, but usually in vain, and never get involved in any spiritual activities like weekend ministries or volunteer groups.

Many clichés come to mind when discussing judgment, such as "make sure your house is clean first before being critical of someone else's mess," or "those who live in glass houses shouldn't cast stones." I'm sure there are others. I'm not sure why I feel like this is such a critical concept for me to grasp, other than the fact that getting a DUI opens the door to humility, criticism, and shame, all of which are driven by society's perception of DUI offenders. I understand this now and can begin to work on becoming a better, more compassionate person.

My mind wanders back to what's being said in class. As I sit listening to the stories, it's clear that some classmates are in better shape than me, some worse. Determined to learn as much as I can from each and every participant, including the counselor, I hope to meet the personal challenges facing me. I want … no, *need*, to be prepared for what lies ahead.

CHAPTER 11

DAY 3: Today was going just fine until now. Earlier I watched the clock pass the hours. No big deal. I blinked my eyes and now, staring at the clock hands as they move with each passing second, I feel my anxiety build in rhythm to the ticks. Like a relaxing vacation, work release time flies … seemingly three times as fast as it does while you are inside. I no longer fear the unknown; the emotion du jour is angst.

I pick up my bunkmate Melissa, and off we go, fully packed and ready for the drive, but leery of what new experiences we may encounter tonight. Yesterday's routine worked well, so we stick with it. Xanax, an Ambien, a swig of water, a turkey wrap followed by a moment of silence to acknowledge the strength that will be needed to get through another night. Praying for heavy eyes after check in. The strip down to one layer is no surprise this time and I'm much more mentally prepared for the invasive frisking. This time the female guard is less "frisky" and leaves some of my personal areas alone. The upper thighs are apparently still fair game, however. I wait for Melissa to get her ten-second full body massage and we head off to our tent.

When we get to our tent, we all exchange hellos. We

have a newbie today. Carlie is in her fifties and in The Tent for fifteen days. Like everyone who enters here, she's very nervous about the process of work release, oversleeping, and how commissary works. I reassure her that we all look out for one another and promise that I will wake her by 6:15 a.m. Once again I rearrange my bunk, doing the best I can to make it comfortable, using that term loosely. The only true comfort I will experience will come on Day 11. Even though it's only eight p.m., I am getting sleepy. The pills are kicking in, thank the good Lord. Trying to avoid mental stimulation of any kind, I flip through a *People* magazine. I hope for a peaceful sleep as my eyes close.

A few hours into my rest, the lights are flicked back on and I awake to the memory that bed checks occur every couple of hours throughout the night. Shit. I totally forgot. I scramble for my ID; the guards only accept IDs from work-release inmates if they are physically handed over. The others just strap their IDs to the bunk posts with hair bands. I forgot to mention this to Carlie and the guard raps on her bunk with her baton and screams at her to produce it. Looking at the fear in her eyes as she stumbles around trying to find her ID, I feel horrible for missing this very important detail in my debriefing.

With the whole ordeal completed, the inmates begin to settle in. It's fascinating to listen as the noise level slowly and steadily dies down to where only a few inmates are repositioning themselves in preparation for the night's rest. Never have I been in a "bedroom" with so many people trying to get some rest at the same time. I can't even think of another situation where this could occur. Girls' summer camp or military boot camp, maybe … but I never went to either of those.

This time I'm prepared to be woken shortly after falling asleep. My rest is very light and as I turn to look at the clock, it reads one a.m. Crap! Did I sleep through the midnight bed check? I look around and there are others awake and bewildered. We all think we missed bed check. After a moment, we calm down. There's no way we all slept through it. No one saw a thing, which takes a bit of the panic out of the equation. The guards must be running late or maybe they're skipping it altogether. Calmer but awake now, I decide to read a little to make myself sleepy.

The guard finally arrives at our tent at 1:20 a.m. Before she takes two steps inside, she begins a screaming rampage at one of the inmates who's lying on a bunk with no mattress. "Get back to your assigned bunk! How stupid are you anyway? Follow the rules or I will roll you up and ship you to where the murderers and rapists hang out!"

"I couldn't see anything when I came in, so I just grabbed an open bunk," she says, quivering with each word.

"Do you think I give a shit?" the guard says. "Why didn't you just turn on the lights? My God, you are as dumb as the day is long!"

What is this, a grade school playground argument? It's now clear that she was released from intake after dark, entered the tent and had no clue as to where to go because she couldn't see a thing … as if the new inmate knows where the light switch is in the total darkness of the night. These pointless point/counterpoint verbal exchanges between the inmates and guards happen regularly. The guards either lack the ability to bring reason to a situation, or they just don't care to. Telling a newbie who just cleared intake in the middle of the night, in total darkness, that she should have turned on the lights in a tent she's never been in is like yelling at your dog for peeing on the floor when there's a perfectly good door it should have opened to let itself out. It's hard enough finding your bunk during the day, let alone at night for the first time. I offer to help the woman make up her bed, but she declines. She tells me that she is only in for twenty-four hours.

It was bitter cold the night before. All through the night everyone commented on how cold they were. I had three layers of clothing, two pairs of socks, four blankets and I was still cold. I woke up a little before six a.m. and decided to run laps around the yard just to get my extremities circulating and my core temperature up. As I put on my shoes, I notice that the newbie is still asleep on top of the dingy, filthy mattress. She will be gone by the time I get back tonight.

I return from my walk and go inside the tent to wake up a couple of the women that I know have the same release time as me. We all brush our teeth, make our bunks, and prepare for our trip to the exit gate. If we show up around 6:30 a.m. maybe we can be out before 7 a.m. I tell the newbie—never did get her name—that she can borrow my phone to call her husband and give him directions as to where to pick her up. As I exit the gate I look over my shoulder and notice, for the first time, the sign that's posted. It reads "Maricopa Sheriff: Con-Tent. Sheriff Joe Arpaio." Clever. Unlike the previous two mornings, there are no helicopter sounds, nor do I remember hearing any in the night. As Melissa and I begin our walk to my truck, we discuss the horns that honk all night long from the semis that drive past. The kind I used to hear when passing a trucker as a kid, and doing the honk-honk signal by pumping my bent arm out the window. Those honks go on all night long. Clearly it's intentional. The jail is famous and an easy target for those who get a kick out of disturbing the peace. I equate it to a car driver who honks his horn just as a golfer is in his backswing. Small kicks for small minds, I guess.

As we drive off, my mind begins to focus on how to get my Ambien and Xanax through the pat-down for the upcoming weekend. I'm still convinced that there is no way I will make it for sixty hours in the elements, with no food and no sleep. If I can somehow sleep a majority of the time, I think I can avert complete boredom and hunger. Reading, walking the yard, maybe some sunbathing … something to take my mind off of the clock. One day at time ….

Home and safe. For a few hours anyway.

* * *

Sixteen Hours of Class Time to Go

I look forward to the alcohol awareness classes now. With several class hours behind me and only sixteen more to go, my mood is changing. Because my license is suspended and I'm determined not to ask for rides, I saddle up on my peddle cruiser and head down the canal trail to my next class. It's only a two mile bike ride and the weather cooperates most days. Bike time allows me to think and plan how to get back the life I once had, or at least a cleaner version of it. With each trip I think of ways to change. Today my ride has me thinking about my social network and circles. I would have to say that they are enablers for the most part. My "church" group of acquaintances really just provides me with justification for my afternoon drinking habits. They are there, so I feel better about being there. I don't think I even have any of their numbers if I wanted to call them to chat. Not that I would.

I'm not that close to any of them. Work friends are a bit more reliable, but even they seemingly focus on finding a good bar to get shitfaced in when they're on the road. A precious few of my friends have it together and stay involved in my life even when it's darkest. I think I will turn my attention to them for a while.

I lock up my bike on the no parking sign outside of the office building where the classes are held, eager to get inside and absorb all the new knowledge. I am very comfortable in the classroom these days. Everyone here is in the same schooner I'm in, and we're all looking for the same answers. They come in the form of opinions, experiences, facts, laws, the "system," the corruption. Imagine one big bitch session with a lesson to be learned at the end. I look forward to seeing familiar faces and love hearing the stories. Classes give me hope that if I can get through this, I can get through anything. Let's face it; this isn't the worst thing that could happen to me. It only feels like it at the moment.

The only way to learn from the classroom experience is to speak up. Get any and all things off your chest if it relates to your DUI, or for that matter, address any issues that deal with addiction and the resulting behavior. Some of our discussion topics are chosen by Mick and other days, he lets us choose the topic. A beefy guy in a flannel shirt in the front row speaks up today, wanting to talk about all of the additional crap that comes with a DUI conviction.

"What's your name?" Mick asks, raising his eyebrows.

"Jeremy."

"Okay, Jeremy, let's start with one issue that's bugging you."

"I guess the main one for me is the license suspension and the insurance requirements." I think: what insurance requirements?

"That's two issues," Mick grinningly says as everyone smiles and chuckles, "but for the purposes of this discussion and in consideration of the time we have today, we'll lump them together. So briefly tell the class how you wound up here and what specifically about the suspension and insurance is causing you issues."

Jeremy goes on to explain his situation. He was coming home from a Scottsdale nightclub around one a.m. and within thirty seconds of leaving the club in his car, he was pulled over. He's definitely not too happy about the cop waiting outside the nightclub parking lot in anticipation of catching would-be drunk drivers. He has a problem with the thirty-day hard license suspension and sixty-day work-only driving permit thereafter. Mick clearly disagrees, but lets Jeremy express his viewpoint. I'm torn between the two opposing views. Like Jeremy, I'm not happy that I have to rely on others or my bike to get around right now. Especially for the first offense. On the other hand, I've come to accept that what I did was pretty egregious, even though it seemed harmless at the time. Is the suspension length really that out-of-line? Let's all just accept the law and move on.

Mick launches into an explanation of what SR22 insurance is and how it works. News to me. Was I just supposed to instinctively know this? I immediately blame my shoddy lawyer. It's his job to explain my responsibilities after a conviction. Mick explains that SR22 is not an insurance policy, despite the name it's been given. SR22 is a document required of high risk drivers by the state as proof of financial liability—or simply put, proof that you have liability coverage with an insurance company. I'm confused. I have to carry this "insurance," even though it's not insurance, for three years?

Looks like I'm going to have to study up on this one. I'm sure it's expensive, like everything else.

The rest of the class turns into a bitch session, only the regular attendees do most of the bitching. Mick is quite good at picking up on our needs … and picking out the newcomers. They have that "fear of the unknown" look, the one that I probably had my first couple of classes. I'm sure that everyone has their own how-and-when agendas when it comes to the court-mandated hours. For some, it's about fitting it into their work schedules; for others, money or convenience. Transportation and jail time come into play too. But most just don't want to be here and view the process as another box to check.

Class ends and I head outside, past the smokers, and hop on my bike to head back home. For me, it's all about the humiliation of riding a bike as opposed to driving, but today, I don't feel like everyone is staring at me, wondering if I'm riding my bike because I have a DUI. It's a beautiful day and many bikers are out on the roads and trails. Today I'm just like any Arizonan enjoying the great weather and soaking in the sunshine.

CHAPTER 12

AY 4: The drive to jail is once again fraught with the anxiety of fighting rush hour traffic, coupled with the fear of being late. It's unbearable. Most of the women I have spoken with tell me they experience the same feeling. Melissa arranged for another ride so I am commuting solo. I arrive with about ten minutes to spare, so I scarf down my turkey wrap and take a swallow of water to wash it down. Before I get out of my truck to check back in, I hear a helicopter overhead. I am so tempted to give Sheriff Joe the one-finger salute as he proudly flies overhead, but instead just ignore this obvious scare tactic. So humiliating. The check in and pat-downs are almost identical to last night's, helping me formulate my drug smuggling plan. Sounds worse when I hear my mind say it this way. Southern Arizona is on the news regularly because of our unsecure borders and the drug wars in Mexico. A better way to describe my plan might be "sneaking" or maybe "covert operation." Yeah, I like that. Sounds official and full of intrigue.

Once I am settled into the tent, my anxiety wears off and dissipates more quickly than in past nights. No newbies tonight ... just my familiar bunkmates. Very little is said this evening. I arrange my bunk and flip through a magazine. Even after commissary opens for the women, I have no desire to go near it. The smell of chow still lingers in the air. There's no chance in hell I could identify what was served earlier in the evening, nor do I want to guess, owing to the connection shared by my mind and stomach.

Putting down my magazine, I stare at the multitude of women flocking over to commissary, returning with handfuls of snacks. Like stoners loading up at a convenience store. Grandma Mary, as any grandmother would, insists that I have some of her snacks. I respectfully decline, but appreciate the gesture. Word of my boycott has spread across the tent and now she's worried about me not eating. Before I settle in for the night's sleep, I visit the lovely and fragrant bathroom facilities. For some reason half the toilets have plastic over them and a sign that reads "do not use." No "out of order" sign or appearance of mechanical failure. Probably just another torture tactic. All of the full toilet paper rolls are kept on a chain and locked up—meaning they can be seen but are inaccessible. All that's left in the stalls are empty rolls. Just when you think it couldn't get any worse. If not for the random piece of facial tissue in my pocket, I would have been forced to get creative.

While we're not allowed to bring pens or pencils into the yard, we can purchase, through the vending machines, colored pencil boxes like the ones you would buy for your child's first day of school. Before I walk back to my tent, I use a colored pencil I borrowed from my friend Melissa to write down the company name and serial numbers of one of the vending machines. After I get home tomorrow morning, I want to test my theory that the vending machines are part of Sheriff Joe's outside business ventures.

Just outside of my tent, I introduce myself to a lady who arrived a day before me. While she isn't staying in my tent, I have seen her walking a lot and talking to some of my tent mates. Gloria is in for 120 days for her second DUI offense—this time an extreme, which means she blew over a 0.15% BAC—with no work release and, because of the Scottsdale arrest, no house arrest option. She's a physical therapist—or was—and in her late fifties. Classy … reminds me of the women I pass by in Scottsdale Fashion Square Mall or at Barnes & Noble. Her attorney costs are in excess of twelve thousand dollars and, with the imposed fines, she is deep in debt and trying to make payments. It's a bit tough, as she puts it mildly, when you're not working. If it weren't for her ex-husband looking after her dogs and home, she wouldn't know who to turn to. She has alienated her friends and family because she just can't convince herself to be honest with them about her conviction. No one knows where she is and, while it is hard for her to shut them out, she prefers it this way. It only proves DUIs can happen to anyone. They destroy lives.

The perfect mix of sleep aids in my system, I am drowsy the moment I lie down. The night should pass quickly.

* * *

Classes with Mick are over and because of those classes, I truly believe that I am much more prepared for jail and all of the other crap associated with it. Mick has a great saying that he uses from time to time. "Welcome to Arizona! Come here for vacation, leave on probation!" I always shake my head and grin when I think about this … Not because I like to see lives ruined or, at the very least, interrupted or inconvenienced. I really do sympathize with their situation. It's more about the clever way the phrase sums up the DUI laws in a state where tourism in the winter is a critical part of the economy. I cannot believe the number of people that I met in these classes that don't even live in AZ. Minnesota, Wisconsin, Colorado, New York … the list goes on. And I will never forget the old Irish/Canadian winter visitor with a big chip on his shoulder. He hated our state with a passion and couldn't wait to finish all his penalty hours, just so that he could get in his car and start driving back to Canada, "flipping off AZ in his rearview mirror," as he so eloquently put it. He literally wore his attitude on vulgar t-shirts in class:

"The Only Job I Need Is a Blow Job!"

"Practice Safe Sex. Go Fuck Yourself!"

I assumed from reading his clothing that he was a lonely, angry old man. He definitely had some entertainment value, I'll give him that. His story was just one of many. Several underage kids, mortgage brokers, real estate agents, musicians, college students, a pregnant teen, nurses, flight attendants … every walk of life, all brought together for the same reason. As the end of the thirty-six hours approached, I knew I would miss the sense of belonging.

Mick is working on starting a program called "Changes," so I put myself on his email list and will probably check it out if it ever comes to fruition. Every person in these classes, every counselor, touches my heart and soul in some resounding way. I'd like to think I could educate friends, family, and co-workers about the laws in AZ, but I'm only one person with one story. Most people don't want to hear it, have heard it before—or worse—and don't believe it could happen to them. Like Mick used to say, "The only safe place to drink alcohol in AZ is in your own home with the blinds closed." Amen to that.

CHAPTER 13

D AY 5: While it's usually me who gets up early and wakes everyone else, this very cold morning I have to be woken up by Melissa. With very little time to spare, I make my bunk and run to the gate, almost missing roll call. This morning they call our tent first, so we are released a little earlier than usual. I am tired even though I had plenty of sleep. I think it is because I'm dreading the coming weekend. Sixty hours of lockup.

The moment I get home I begin my research on the vending machines. All I can come up with is that the phone number is linked to a Coca-Cola distributor in town. While this doesn't mean Sheriff Joe is clean of any links to the vendors supplying the jail system, it does mean my limited detective skills cannot make a connection. I drop the idea—too much work and too much of a reminder of where I'm spending my evenings.

Maybe we all revert to our infancy when faced with emotional stress. It seems that way for Melissa, who texts me at 2 p.m., saying that she is stressed and only wants to cry, eat and sleep. No surprise—the afternoon is once again an anxious one, although for me, this day's anxiety is fed by thoughts of my covert operation at intake. Today is the day I need to figure out how to get my sleep aids into the prison for the weekend. I've been searched enough now and have a pretty good idea of what they pat down and what body parts they stroke. Still, the thought of getting caught makes me sick to my stomach. I imagine that they'd immediately take work release away and roll me—put me into stripes and extend my sentence. I spend the afternoon trying to figure out a way to "test run" some pills into the yard.

Of all people, my mother's idea makes the most sense. I didn't know she has it in her! Take a waterproof bandage that has adhesive on all four sides, and put a couple of pills in the center where the pad of the bandage is. Place it right above my crotch—at the hair line, center. My jeans, especially in that region, are thick and the zipper area is padded. The perfect hiding place! Barring a random strip search, I think this will work. Let's give it a shot.

I pick up Melissa and fill her in on the plan. She insists I'm a lunatic but likes the idea and wants to see how the first run goes before opting in. Even though she doesn't depend on drug-induced sleep like I do, she relishes the idea of napping her way through the weekend without a whole lot of effort.

Nervous and tense don't begin to describe my inner state as Melissa and I head toward the intake doors. I remove my sweatshirt, down to my t-shirt and jeans. The pat-down begins. First the armpits, then back, rear end, and finally up each leg. I hope that's it. Nope. The guard reaches around my waist and I feel my nerves trigger my upper body into a quiver. Please don't wonder if anything is unusual today. Please don't feel any mysterious bumps below my waistline. Please … Before I am able to turn around in full expectation that I'll be asked to unbutton and unzip my pants, I am released and told to pick up my things and head inside. Success! Once inside, I hide the pills in my flashlight battery compartment. The flashlight stays in my bunk area with my books, water bottle and extra socks. Tomorrow night I'll wear a bigger bandage, and bring the rest of the party favors in. Only Melissa is in on the caper—no one else. I can't take the chance that the guards will overhear conversations about this. Besides, I really don't trust my new friends. Melissa is even a stretch. I don't know them that well and fear being thrown under the bus, rolled up and put into stripes.

Night time is uneventful. In bed early, I pick up the same magazine I've read ten times and page through it in case there's an article I previously skipped over. Some of the other women are playing cards and visiting. All is peaceful as I quickly fall into a heavy slumber. I hope someone else rolls down and secures the tent sides tonight. It won't be me.

* * *

Traffic Survival School

With the alcohol awareness classes finished, my attention turns toward completing my required traffic survival school. After spending thirty-six hours in a classroom setting, this should be a breeze. I just need to get through these last eight hours and I will have completed all of my required class work. Amen. Unlike Mick's classes, this one will probably be a tedious eight hours filled with stupid comments from angry speeders and red light runners. Phoenix and Scottsdale are two of the first cities in the nation to implement the controversial photo radar program, designed to catch law breakers when traffic cops aren't waiting in the bushes. In lieu of paying the fine and losing points for a traffic offense, a driver can elect to pay for a class, sit through eight hours of instruction, and keep their points intact. If I had to guess, I'd say the state has had to add many days to the traffic survival school schedule because of the photo radar system. Another state money maker. It cost me $55, but the added ticket fines and the cost of the class for misdemeanor offenses are well over $100 per incident. I guess it's the one and only time I feel like I got off easy.

With my final class scheduled for tomorrow, I sit down with my DUI folder, which looks and feels more like a home mortgage portfolio, and begin to tally up the costs thus far. I must have calculated incorrectly. I know that the sum was going to be exorbitant, but this can't be right. I write it all down and run it through my calculator one more time.

$150.00 towing charge—to Scottsdale PD for administration fees
$465.01 towing charge—mandatory 30-day storage fee
$250.00 court fine
$210.00—84% surcharge on the court fine
$47.60 sentence enhancement
$500.00 DUI assessment
$500.00 DPS assessment
$34.00 reimbursement to Scottsdale PD for blood sample procedures
$841.00 jail fees for the 10 days
$5,000.00 for the attorney
$60.00 for alcohol/drug screening
$240.00 for alcohol/drug classes
$1,050.00 Interlock device at $75/month for 1 year

+ $75 each for install/uninstall
$1,948.32 for SR22 insurance at $54.12/month
for 3 years
$12.00 Arizona Identification Card
$32.00 License Reinstatement Fee
$55.00 Traffic Survival School

My calculator reads $11,394.93. Over eleven grand in expenses that could have been avoided by leaving the beer at home. I begin to cry as suicidal thoughts creep into my head. No. I refuse to take the easy way out. No matter how difficult this is, I will find a way to get through it. The financial burden is overwhelming, on top of all my regular expenses. With two credit cards maxed out, I just stare out my sliding glass doors. I make pretty good money but will still struggle to get this paid off in any reasonable time period. How do others with little or no income weather the storm? I guess the state allows for an individual to make payments for the fines, but there are so many other expenses that require full payment up front. Granted, my largest expense—an attorney—was a complete waste of money, at least for my situation.

Hoping to clear my head, I head out the door with the dogs for a long run. Get through tomorrow, check off the box, and move on to the next phase.

CHAPTER 14

DAY 6: Up earlier than usual this morning, I decide to walk the yard. About a hundred men in stripes on the other side of the chain link fence are walking in twos toward a set of buses. One can only venture a guess where they are headed. Sheriff Arpaio revived chain gangs as part of his incarceration tactics, so maybe they are off to clean up a roadside somewhere. It's breezy, but not bitterly cold like the past mornings. The dust periodically kicks up with the gusts, and the tents sway under the wind's control. It dawns on me that the guards have tamed their antics during the nights. Or is it that I'm just sleeping through them now, numb to their ridiculous interruptions? I'm not sure. Whatever the reason, I'm getting better sleep than at first and my days back at home seem more productive.

I finish my walk and head to the bathroom to brush my teeth. The prison-issued toothpaste is horrible. Feeling confident in my covert abilities, I decide to take a tube of it home, empty it out, and fill it with my own toothpaste. A gang-banger type girl is standing at one of the sinks washing her underwear with the crappy hand soap and some unidentified makeshift scrub brush. I try not to look over, but can't help it. Okay. So there are multiple uses for the jail issued feminine pads; incarceration inspires creativity. At least she's resourceful. I really don't need to see the panties hanging off the side of the sink as she walks away to use the toilet. Vicki's Secret they're not. Thanks for the visual. This story definitely needs to be shared with my tent mates. I get back and, after I tell the story of the panty-laundering gang banger, I bust out in laughter as Grandma Mary tells the group that Mob Mom uses the feminine pads to dry her hands! No paper towels or hand dryers at our disposal, so I guess the rule is to make do with what you have. This place grows more disgusting each day I'm here.

It is going to be a hot ninety degrees over the weekend. At times during the day there is no shade anywhere to be found and, since it is required that the tent be rolled up during the day, the afternoon sun just beats down on us. The plan is to wear shorts underneath my jeans tonight and take extra panties in for my sixty hour stay.

"I'm really worried about you … you're so skinny to begin with and you never eat while you're here. How are you going to survive the weekend?" Grandma Mary says in a sympathetic tone.

"The morning oranges and bread will be enough," I tell her. "Don't worry. I plan on bringing in two rolls of quarters for emergency purposes." I brief Melissa about controlling my money after my nightly dose of Ambien, because I am weak and will want to spend it when the effects begin to kick in.

I am going to taste the food provided at evening chow. Just once, I'd like to try to identify the contents. Hopefully, I won't make myself sick. I can always wash it down with hose water. Melissa and I take off for the exit, eager to get the hell out of here.

Today's hours at home are quiet. The short agenda includes taking one of my dogs to the vet to have her eye infection treated. Guilty, sad, and worried because I will not be there to care for her over the weekend, I nevertheless realize I have no other recourse but to leave her with a friend. It's the flexible schedule that I'm just now realizing I take for granted. If this were any other commitment, I would have just canceled and made sure I would be around for my dog the whole weekend. Calling up the Sheriff's office and rearranging my schedule is not an option, so I'm just going to have to deal with it.

My other short-listed agenda items: washing my jail clothes, getting my pills ready to smuggle in for the weekend, and converting my second jail-issued toothpaste tube into sunscreen. This is going to take some extra time to think through. It is quite a time-consuming project, emptying the rancid toothpaste from the tube and slowly syringing in sunscreen. Since the guards know I check these jail-issued tubes in and out each day, I'm really not worried that they'll examine the contents; sunscreen disguised as toothpaste will easily make it past them for the weekend.

Melissa, in her fragile and anxious state, asks if I am interested in seeing a movie before we check back in—something light and funny to get our minds off everything. Good idea. Besides, I'm a big movie buff, so this should ease my mind.

My brilliant plan has gone terribly wrong. I keep going back to the tents, freaking out at the thought of the guards tossing our bunks during the day when we are all on work release. What if they find the pills hidden in my flashlight? Fuck. I can't even focus on the movie, which, by the way, requires very little concentration—*Dinner for Schmucks*. A total waste of nine bucks. After the movie, we go back to my place, shower and pack our weekend clothes. Melissa's hands are shaking as I hand her a bandage and her pills. After I school her on how and where to apply the bandage, she calms down a bit. The only fear, once again, is that the weekend guards have a different procedure on intake searches. A random strip search would basically wipe out everything we have accomplished up to this point. We load up the truck and leave.

I try to avoid the thought of being caught for any one of the numerous rules we're breaking and have broken already. On our way to jail, I stop at Chipotle to grab dinner. My last real meal for the next sixty hours! Melissa doesn't seem to mind the jail food, so she's not quite as enamored as I am by the big burrito bowls sitting in front of us.

A deep breath precedes my exit from the truck as we march confidently toward the intake doors. One last convincing glance at each other to acknowledge our mutual risk is strangely empowering. I've done the homework and have been successful on the first attempt. What do we have to fear? The confidence quickly turns to nervousness as we go through pat-down. The weekend guard checking us in is luckily no different than the others—no extracurricular reach-arounds or strip searches. We've been cleared and are now officially in for the next sixty hours.

* * *

Two Weeks Until Tent City ...

Traffic survival school goes as expected. Other than a few stupid comments and questions from traffic offenders followed by a couple of videos on common sense rules of the road, the eight hours passes quickly, leaving me with two weeks until the day of incarceration. I've got to get my license situation squared away, and the whole DMV thing is always such a pain in the ass. Even with the simplest of tasks, the DMV workforce makes everything unnecessarily tedious. I can't wait to see how they handle the complexity of a DUI.

My thirty-day hard suspension transitions over today, so it's time to head to the DMV and get my sixty-day work permit. I gather all my DMV "notification of action" letters, arrange a ride with one of my best friends—Mike—and head to the nearest DMV office. Mike has brought a book with him, expecting the wait to extend well into the afternoon. Surprisingly, they call my number in the first fifteen minutes. Without too much humiliation, I sit down and explain my situation to the gentleman behind the desk. I can tell immediately that he's a genuinely nice guy who understands and wants to help. He explains that I am indeed completing my thirty day suspension period, and that there are a few documents that need to be presented in order to obtain the work permit: a certificate of completion for the eight hour traffic survival class, proof of an SR22 insurance policy, and proof that I installed the DMV mandated ignition interlock. Oh … I knew about the ignition interlock requirement, but didn't know I needed it for my work permit. I have everything else but haven't installed the freaking interlock. As I should have expected, a wasted trip to the DMV. I apologize to Mike for dragging me down here only to quickly follow up my apology with another request for a favor. I need to get my truck in to the interlock install place tomorrow. I hope I don't burn through all of my favors on this.

* * *

Because I'm still on a hard suspension, Mike needs to drive to my place, bring me up to the interlock installation place, take me to the DMV, and then drive with me back to my house to get his car so he can go home. The guilt weighs heavily on my mind—it's like lying to the Pope. Mike has always had enormous patience with me and, likewise, I would do anything for the guy. Sensing my guilt, he reminds me of the countless times I've helped him out of a jam or took on some crappy job to lighten his load. He also was the one who prodded me to ask Lucky out and that disastrous decision alone tends to even the score, if ever there was one. The relationship works.

Eight authorized installation companies in the valley provide me with a little bit of choice as to where to go. I've never heard of any of them, so I pick the one closest to the DMV location where we'll be heading right after. Yesterday I set the appointment for 10:00 a.m. and Mike, a punctuality freak, rings my doorbell at 9:15 a.m. for a twenty minute drive. We bug out and grab a coffee, my treat. A few laughs along the way make the trip a little less painful. After all, I'm going to be blowing into this thing every time I want to drive. Not a very pleasant thought. In an industrial park garage tucked away in relative obscurity, we're greeted by two men who look better suited to working at a stolen car chop shop than for a state agency contracted supplier. It's evident that they, like trained monkeys, have a strict procedural process that they are required to follow, right down to what they are and aren't allowed to say. The install guys exude just enough professionalism to keep me from walking out; their eyes say, "Thanks for keeping our doors open by being an idiot DUI offender." Then again, I'm still trying to work through this issue of caring what others think of me, so maybe their disdain is only in my mind. Mike and I are led to a small room with a table and TV/VCR combo. While they complete the install, I'm instructed—as part of the process—to watch a video on the operation of the contraption.

After forty-five minutes of impatient aggravation, I am called out of the waiting room. The install is complete. I'm told that I have to sign a binding contract and that if I don't, there will be a $250 cancellation fee. Seems entirely backwards to me. Shouldn't the contract come first? I have no choice and want to get the hell out of there, so I sign. And so, training begins. Mike and I can't help but laugh at what's required to get a successful blow. The unit operates with air pressure and sound, so I have to blow steadily while humming at a certain pitch. It's tricky, especially doing it and stifling laughter at the same time. Knowing we're not getting out of here without three successive passing blows, I concentrate. After ten more minutes, we're backing out of the garage and on our way to the DMV.

Mike, present more for support than as my chauffer, hangs out in the seating area again and waits for me to repeat the DMV process. A longer wait this time. Finally, I am called up to the same window as last time. Luckily, the same man is behind the desk. He doesn't remember me but is just as friendly as before. He flips through my paperwork and tells me everything looks good. He then takes a hole punch, clamps down on my original driver's license, and hands it back to me along with a temporary paper permit. The kind you get when you first learn to drive. "This will serve as your license for the next sixty days. If you're pulled over, show the officer this paper and you should be good. This permit only allows you to drive to and from work, doctor appointments, and any state-mandated class or detention. Drive for any other purpose and the permit can be revoked, leaving you with a hard suspension for the remaining days."

"Okay, thanks," I humbly reply.

He then advises me to get an Arizona identification card, since my driver's license can no longer be used as ID. I mentally add this little snippet of advice to my 'humiliated' column.

He explains that, after my sixty day restricted permit period is over, I can apply for a regular license, the only difference being the words INTERLOCK in big letters stamped across it. Might as well stamp "LOSER" across my forehead, too, while you're at it. If I get caught driving any vehicle that does not have an interlock during my one year sentence, I will be cited for driving with a suspended license. More court time, more jail time, license revocation, and mounds of costs. I won't risk it.

I take the truck straight home from the DMV and make peace with the fact that I will have to use the device for the next year if I want to drive anywhere. As I wipe down my bicycle, I mentally chart all the restaurants and convenience stores within walking or biking distance. Driving will be inevitable, but reducing the number of times I have to drive will help the environment … and help me avoid the humiliation of climbing into my truck in a parking lot and having others around me see this device in my mouth as I blow, waiting for it to give me the green light.

CHAPTER 15

DAY 7: "Attention Con-Tents, kick-outs get to the gate." Startled by this loudspeaker broadcast—It's nearly midnight after all—I try to make sense of it. Why are they getting kicked out? What did they do? Last names follow the general announcement. I shake off a few more cobwebs and start putting it together. They are calling the inmates that are scheduled to be released in the morning. Getting kicked out, as it happens, is a good thing. "Bring your personal belongings and linens. You are getting kicked out!" Wow … any time you can be released early from this place is a Godsend. I hope that when it's my turn, I am released several hours early.

Our tent is almost full. Several girls moved in during the dark and creepy night. In my sleepy state, I did my best to help them find mattresses and make up their bunks. It's a definite reminder of my luck at being admitted during daylight hours.

The anticipation of this morning's commissary provides comic relief from this otherwise sad and tragic situation. The vending machines have been stocked overnight and, as a result, a massive line has formed, wrapping around the building. The female inmates, arms crossed and shivering, wait impatiently for their turn to stock up on junk food for the weekend. Most of the inmates understand that the machines are usually empty by Saturday night and that there is only a remote possibility that the guards will refill them. I watch as each woman leaves the area with handfuls of potato chip bags and other mysterious food products, heading back to her bunk area to store her weekend stash.

Even though I'm aware that it's going to be a long weekend, I resist spending the money. The breakfast options consist of oranges, bread, "mystery meat," and milk. I'm hungry, but can only manage to eat an orange. The bread has a very strange smell and taste and it is unusually weighty. The rumor is that it is baked especially for the jail, with extra yeast. I don't know if the rumor's true or what the purpose of this recipe change would be, other than one more ploy by Sheriff Joe to make this place as disgusting as possible. Regardless, the women eat it and even buy tuna out of the vending machines to make sandwiches. I take a pass on the bread today.

Mainly to kill time, Melissa and I do laundry. I can justify spending money for clean clothes. The washer and dryer are outside, next to the soda machines. They are basic appliances that look to be very old—like ones you might find on Craigslist for about fifty bucks a set. If we combine our efforts, we can get our socks and towels washed for half the cost. Melissa was down to her last buck fifty, but after sharing her quandary at morning commissary, one of the "kick-outs" gave her five bucks, saying she didn't need it. Sharing her newfound wealth, she buys me a grape soda—which tastes like a little slice of heaven—and contributes a portion of the remaining cash to laundry.

Both of us hear something come across the loudspeaker but shrug it off. We have been tuning out the nonsense and idle threats that dominate the airwaves. Strangely, I see a small wave of women walking back to the tents as if directed to do so. I have a slight panic attack; I don't need to fall victim to unintentional disobedience. One of the women approaches and warns us that lockdown is in ten minutes. Missing lockdown ... who knows what the penalty is for such a despicable crime? Leaving our laundry, we head back to our bunks and wait. The on-duty guard that day is unfamiliar. We immediately nickname her "Bangs"—her hair is pulled back and has ridiculously short bangs that curl under. Looks about twelve years old. Super bitch. With an ego the size of Everest, she orders us to get rid of the bottles that we have filled with rocks to use as our personal free weights. "Dis is jail, not yo' local LA Fitness," she screams in an undeterminable dialect and accent. She also makes us get rid of the bottles of Clorox, which serve a dual purpose. They are used by the long-timers who have to clean the bathrooms as part of their duties, but others use them to sanitize their mattresses. She's not done yet. All of the towels and blankets that hang on the bunk bed bars to block the scorching sun during the day must be taken down; she claims they are a fire hazard. Unless they've had problems in the past with spontaneous fires popping up in jail—where no matches or lighters are allowed—I don't think towels hanging on bed bars can contribute to, stoke, or start a fire. Chalk it up to another ridiculous nonsensical explanation to make this place even less tolerable. After scurrying around to meet the ludicrous demands of Bangs, we are told that lockdown is lifted and return to the laundry area.

Morning gives way to early afternoon and, after washing our things and attempting to dry them in the useless dryer, we hang our clothes over the bed supports. Yes, I know that we are risking a tent fire, but we feel particularly rebellious today. I'm finding out that this place is much easier to take if you have a pal to hang with, so Melissa and I again team up to wash our faces in the bathroom with shampoo we got from Mob Mom. Pathetically, we use the feminine napkins as washcloths and hand towels … Washing my face with a shampoo-laced maxi pad and drying it with a clean one … now that's living! At least we are somewhat clean before applying sunscreen from the toothpaste tube turned applicator that I smuggled in. I change into shorts and sit outside the tent to read. The midday sun is hot and it won't be long before I will be sporting a farmer's tan.

This time I hear the loudspeaker blurt out the lock-down and head-check, so I close my book and go back in. "The Sleeper," a girl who appears only on the weekends, is now located across from my bunk; whereas last weekend she slept below me on the bottom bunk. I hear she is serving five consecutive weekends, but no one seems to know her status or sentence. She is never awake! I guess she chooses to repress her memories of this place by keeping her conscious hours to a minimum. Our tent is getting regular newbie traffic today and will likely be full by the end of the weekend.

The head-check process takes forever to reach our tent. It's 3 p.m. and our tent just about got "tossed." Earlier today three male guards walked through the yard—unbeknownst to us. They were spying, looking for violators of the vaguely defined tent system. Busted on the inside. The male guards informed the guard on duty that women were outside of Tent 70 sunning themselves. I guess it's a crime to sit in the sun, when the only other options are to sit on your bunk or walk around. I had been sitting on a concrete slab and a couple of girls from another tent were sitting on the partially towel-covered rocks next to me. I guess we are the culprits. The female guard who does the head-check for our tent—"D&G" we call her, due to her fancy sunglasses—reminds us in a screechy, annoying tone that "this is not some beach or your personal tanning salon! If we catch you again, we WILL toss your tent and roll you all into stripes. This is my yard and these are my rocks. I'm the boss and I WILL do whatever I want to do to you while I'm on duty." Okay … she apparently drank a highly caffeinated Big Gulp infused with an ego-boosting powder before she showed up for work today. Evil glares pin me from all corners of the tent. They've identified me as the radical rule-breaker. Whatever.

Tonight is the night I decide to taste the chow, which is rolled out into the middle of the yard in steel carts. Getting in line is a race for some, but I timidly walk toward the serving line. The smell reminds me of a grade-school cafeteria thirty years ago, when school administrators couldn't care less about the quality or content of the food. Meeting a minimum calorie level was all that mattered. I watch hundreds of flies swarm the uncovered food trays. I am handed a tray with a previous night's dinner encrusted in the concave food compartments, making contact with what they call tonight's dinner. Again, it's difficult to discern what the contents are other than a doughnut buried in applesauce. A dessert befitting a … well, a convict, I guess. A plastic spoon, purposely buried under the runny slop that serves as the mystery main course, is the only utensil. More in-depth study reveals that the special du jour is a bread roll drowned in refried beans. I am handed two half-pints of milk. I taste-test each item, gagging and dry-heaving on every bite. Nothing really has a distinct flavor, but the smell … the smell is more reminiscent of a high school anatomy dissection class. Ditching my tray on the return rack, I get back in line for a second helping of milk, hoping that each carton will have barter value later in the evening.

I notice that several girls are just now being released into the yard after being in intake since 7 a.m. The borderline torture continues; they are not allowed to have anything to eat until they are assigned to a bunk. Knowing what it's like to enter hungry, I go to my secret stash of bread saved from breakfast and give it to two of the incoming newbies. One of them, Tonya, discloses that she is eighteen and has been sentenced to five days for tagging. I don't ask, but I assume that means graffiti. This is her first time in The Tent. She is a tough-looking African-American who, after our conversation, I realize isn't so tough after all. She has a breakdown and just sits on her bunk crying. The other girl thanks me but says little and otherwise keeps to herself.

Once again, mostly out of sheer boredom, Melissa and I head off to the washing machine to do laundry so that we will have fresh things for Sunday. Our shirts and shorts are sweaty from sitting outside in the heat and, with so few items to wear, it makes sense to clean them regularly. It also kills time. Wise to the futility of using the dryer, we both bring our wet clothes back to our bunks to dry.

Night is falling, so I decide to take a long walk around the campsites to burn time. An unplanned collect call to Mom to check on the dogs breaks up the walk. It's so humiliating listening to the recording asking the receiver of the call if she is willing to accept the charges. No, *embarrassing* is the more appropriate term here … I must live with humiliation for the rest of my life, so using it to describe this situation is inaccurate. She accepts and we talk briefly. I'm really in no mood to chat. At least I hang up knowing that the dogs are fine and huddled on the floor with full bellies and sleepy eyes. Lucky dogs.

Commissary is a bust for everyone this evening. As expected, the vending machines are completely empty. I don't understand why the guards bother to have the inmates stand in line for an hour or more when there is nothing left. Just a way of fucking with us, I'm sure. I've taken my meds for the evening, so I will soon be fast asleep.

* * *

Ten Days Until Tent City

Ten days until I have to report. It's impossible to get my mind off of it. Every time I step foot in my truck, I am reminded. Every time I pull out my credit card and think about the enormous balance, I am reminded. All of my requirements outside of jail have been completed. The countdown begins.

I don't feel like starting any projects until after my sentence, so I just sit with nothing to do except let my mind wander into dark places. I'm sure that when I look back at this, it will seem like a very small moment in time, but as of right now, I am mortified by what could possibly be the biggest event in my life. Carrying the permanent stigma of "DUI offender" takes the form of an enormous tumor in my mind. Some days it makes me dizzy and nauseated; other days I just cry. A huge knowledge gap exists between the general population who have avoided DUI convictions and those who have gone through the process. It's a little like experiencing a sudden death in the family when you've never lost a family member or close relative before: you can't know how it will affect you until it happens, and it changes you forever. A major difference is that engaging in reckless drinking and driving behavior is a choice and can be avoided.

I think about the next series of options quite often now. If I have driven somewhere out for the evening, I can a) have a drink and risk another DUI by driving myself home, b) have a drink and call a cab or a friend to get me home and back to my car the next day, or c) choose not to drink. I can honestly say that I will struggle with all three of these options. The decision will be easy at first, since I will not be able to drive under these conditions while I have the interlock device. My actions, after the device has been removed, however, will define how well I handle the situation. I'd like to say that one year with the interlock is enough to change my habits. Truth is, I don't know. I still drink, and drinking affects judgment, so in my sober state, I am concerned about what I might do.

I think I will put in a bunch of work hours up until a couple of days before reporting to prison. Sitting around home thinking about my situation would surely send me spiraling into depression. I have access to far too many things around here that can kill me and, with my history, it's best to spend the next several days away.

CHAPTER 16

DAY 8: As expected, our tent is filling up with new arrivals, who had to find their way through the maze of tents in the middle of the night. I must be adjusting to the noise, because my sleep is hardly disturbed … whispers, whimpers, mattresses being pulled from one bunk, dragged, and placed on another. If I hear them, I no longer get up, falling quickly back to sleep. They are on their own.

I am up early this morning, before everyone else in my tent. After grabbing my book, I walk the yard trying to find a little spot away from everything to do some reading. I see my friend Gloria (from Tent 64, in her late fifties and serving 120 days) outside of her tent. She waves me over. "Good morning," she says. "Would you mind grabbing an extra bag at breakfast if you don't see me in line? I have been sleeping terribly and need to lie back down."

I agree, but then quickly become aware that grabbing a second bag at breakfast puts me at risk of getting caught. Who knows what sort of mood the guards will be in today? The heat in Arizona makes everyone a little crazy after a while, but in Tent City you've got a strange, hierarchical mix of inmates and guards all having to coexist. The capture of a two-bagged inmate coupled with the heat could set off a whole string of repercussions. Still, unable to say no, I let her know that I will bring it to her bunk.

Round one of breakfast—consisting of bread, oranges, and two half-pints of milk—is rolled out into the yard, and I get in line with all the other girls. I quickly grab my bag, bring it to my bunk area, and nervously get back in line for Gloria's bag. Apparently Mob Mom has the same idea, but lacks any fear, for she is also back in line, right in front of me. "Take out your ponytail and shake your hair. They won't even notice." Leave it to Mob Mom to know how to work the system. My second time through the line goes quickly and without a hitch, my double-bagging episode a success. Anytime we can pull one over on the guards feels like a victory for the insiders. With Gloria fast asleep, I set her breakfast bag and milk next to her, quietly slip away, and head back to my bunk to eat.

It doesn't take long for Mob Mom to see my sunburned shoulders and offer up her lotion. I am continuously surprised and impressed by the generosity regularly on display around here. There is a heightened feeling of mutual respect and admiration for which I'm extremely grateful. The kindness of the inmates reduces the constant anxiety and loneliness that this place fosters. Without the instant friendships based on our similar circumstances and the need to unite against the guards, the isolation would be unbearable.

After breakfast, I find Melissa and we hang out and talk. She has been having a hard time reassembling her life since she was convicted. Her close friends drifted away because she began distancing herself. She couldn't share her shameful story. She has no boyfriend to speak of—just friends with benefits. Even those relationships have started to grow strained from her isolating behavior. Having dropped out of

ASU shortly after enrolling, she is lost and really has nowhere to turn. I feel sorry for her. No matter how bad you think you have it, someone else has it worse. In just the eight days I've been here, I've found out how devastating a DUI can be.

Melissa suggests braiding my hair so I let her. Just another way to quell the boredom. I'm embarrassed by my dirty hair, but I quickly get over that and turn my attention to how I'd like it braided. With shoulder-length hair, my options are limited. A French braid is the only way to go. We end our conversation and I sit, quiet and motionless, while she braids. Knowing that she is running out of money for commissary, I pay her three dollars. Our private economy is modest, but it works.

The day makes its turn toward the afternoon as the tent's temperature continues its rapid ascent. It's a good time to roll up the sides of the tent and let whatever air there is blow through. The tents have undoubtedly never been washed. They are filthy from the outside elements and stink to high heaven. The only way to roll up the sides of the tent without allowing the permanent stench of the tent flaps to get on your hands is to wear the rubber gloves from the bathroom. These are the same gloves used by the stripes to do their nightly cleaning of the lavatories. I'm trading stinky tent smell for sweaty inmate hand smell from the gloves—a crude metaphor for my life's tradeoffs.

As time ticks by, we are eventually treated to some ice in our water barrel. There is too much ice to squeeze into the barrel, so the guards dump the overflow onto the ground. I'm not sure if I'm too proud or too lazy, but I choose not to participate in the mad scramble to both the barrel for cool water and the ice on the ground. Makeshift ice packs are created with towels, socks, and spare tops, while some ice chunks are dropped down shirts for instant cooling.

Commissary is a nightmare this afternoon. The only reason I go is to observe and to visit with girls from other tents. I still fight the urge to spend money on the inside. Two of the vending machines are acting up. One is eating quarters and only accepting dollar bills. The other is accepting dollars bills, but only one bill. The quarters just fall through to the change compartment. If one of the items is over a dollar, the machine won't disperse it. All the girls who want tuna, chicken or lunchables are S.O.L. Of course, it isn't a democracy in here, so no one should be surprised at the signs posted on the machines that state, "Buy at your own risk, no refunds." It's hard to imagine how much money is lost in those machines every day. In the outside world, a kick, a shake, and a few swear words are typically in order for a vending machine that malfunctions. You can report the malfunction to the store owner. On the inside, however, you wouldn't dare touch the machines outside the parameters of the buttons. Walk away pissed off and frustrated, but just walk away. When the machines are working, they allow for some fascinating, creative food combinations and meal preparations. The recipe would read something like this:

> One bag pre-cooked chili
> One bag Fritos
>
> Heat chili bag on a midsummer day's Arizona rock for 20 minutes. Open both bags, dump the Fritos into the chili bag and enjoy. Serves one.

Tragic, but immensely resourceful.

Mob Mom is in the final week of her six-month stay in

The Tent. She has been on work furlough, which apparently is different from work release. In addition to jail fines, work furlough inmates who are typically incarcerated for thirty days or more have to give the jail one hour of their pay, plus three dollars per day for the privilege of being released for work. Copies of their pay stubs are required for proof of income and employment. Taking into account these additional charges, the multitude of collected fines, and vending machine revenue, I would be surprised if the county has to kick in any taxpayer money to keep this place open for business.

I finally toughen up Melissa and convince her to start charging girls to braid their hair. She doesn't mind doing it because it kills time, but I tell her that if she charges something minimal, she can use it for sodas or water. Depending on whether or not she knows the girls, she charges twenty-five to fifty cents. This afternoon she is thrilled to have made a dollar fifty, enough to buy a soda. My vending machine boycott is still in effect, but I have found a way to flavor the hose water. Taking an orange from breakfast, I squeeze the juice into the bottle I am using—the same one that my bunkmate gave me eight days ago. It doesn't remove the rusty, metallic taste, but it does improve it slightly, enough to make it palatable. These simple little discoveries make time go by a little faster and make this place a touch more tolerable.

As the sun sets on this city within a city, the guards enter our tent and berate us for wearing tank tops in our bunks. They are too revealing. Three girls in our tent are specifically identified this time and threatened to be rolled up—put in stripes and have their work release privileges taken away—if they are found again in tank tops. The guard yesterday said tank tops are okay. Each has his or her own rules and procedures while on duty. It's not unusual for guards to change imposed rules based on their moods. Today we were all ordered to stay out of the shaded areas of the yard and either remain in the sun or in our bunks during the heat of the day. Yesterday sun tanning wasn't allowed. So let me get this straight—sit in the sun but no sun tanning? Some of us in here may not be educated, but we certainly don't operate under logic so twisted that it can only be acceptable to a two-year-old. Common sense takes a back seat to the guards' overinflated egos.

Carlie, one of the work release girls who has checked back into our tent this evening, is in deep shit. During intake, the guards smelled alcohol on her and made her do a blow test. Claiming that she had only one glass of wine at lunchtime, she has been ordered to her bunk until they decide what to do with her. She's crying and very scared. Giving her a comforting hug, I quickly realize that there's no way she had only one glass of wine at lunch. She reeks of booze. Anyone sentenced for a DUI conviction who would risk reporting to jail smelling of alcohol is most definitely an alcoholic—and needs help. Don't expect a counselor to visit Tent City. About an hour later, her name is called on the loudspeaker and she's ordered to bring all her belongings with her to the office. Rolled up, put in stripes, and work release privileges revoked for the remainder of her stay. I'm sure this is the last I will see of her. Alcoholism is a menacing disease in the outside world, but its psychological and emotional effect can be compounded by a conviction. Because of her addiction, this girl will likely lose her job and now the inability to be released for work. Drinking at lunch during work release is irresponsible. Not seeking help for an addiction leads to further life-destroying behavior.

It has been a busy day of doing nothing. Much to observe with lessons learned. Time for bed, same ritual—swallow pills, drink water, grab magazine and fall asleep. Tomorrow I'll wake up and have only two days and nights left to go—and a lifetime to hold the memory of it.

CHAPTER 17

DAY 9: It's early Monday morning and virtually no one has had a decent night's sleep. Up until now, it seemed that standard procedure called for female guards to come through periodically with flashlights, but last night was much different. Male guards appeared at several intervals throughout the night, flipping on the lights, walking through for no apparent reason, and leaving the lights on after they left. The loudspeaker was constantly going on and off, with no purpose other than to babble something unimportant. It felt like a form of sleep deprivation torture, although we are not in small cells with one table and two chairs, staring into bright lights, being forced to confess. Let them have their fun, I guess. Apparently boredom weighs as heavily on them as it does on us.

I can smell my own stench from two nights and three days of minimal hygiene. Just a couple more hours until I can go home, clean up, and feel human again, if only for a few hours. The majority of the girls don't bother showering here. Only the long-timers, or those who get in with their clothes on to cool off. Girls wash their dirty feet in the bathroom sinks and then splash a little water on their faces and armpits.

Very third world.

I'm exhausted. When the guards weren't keeping me awake, it was the smell: the disgusting odor of unwashed bodies confined within a small space or the unwashed tents themselves. Our discharge time is delayed today because the men were given first release. It's a miserable wait. A horrific smell from the humane society euthanasia building makes its way across the street to the jail. Today is burn day. If the smell and eye irritation isn't enough to make you cry, the thought about what is transpiring over there will.

I have heard that over the weekends vehicles in the parking lot outside of the jail routinely get vandalized. I'm sure it's too much to ask that the busy guards occasionally patrol the parking lot for vandals and thieves. Worried about my truck, which has spent the weekend in the parking lot, I speed-walk to its parking place, as if I might be able to stop an imaginary break-in that is taking place right now in broad daylight. When I finally get to my truck, no one has broken in. After I drop Melissa off, however, I notice handprints all over the passenger side windows. Someone cased my vehicle and at least considered breaking in. During my days in jail I am mentally violated, and now I have to put up with having my possessions targeted. I break down completely, crying all the way home.

* * *

April 10, 2009: The Day Before my Incarceration

Night approaches rapidly and there's no way I'm going to be able to sleep. Tomorrow's date with the county jail system is fully occupying my mind, keeping everything else out. I try to imagine what the next ten nights will be like, but all I can think about is the fact that Tent City is internationally notorious for its terrible conditions. I can't help but imagine and expect the worst. I feel ashamed, sorry for my behavior and for burdening those close to me with my problems. I'm angry at myself for allowing this to happen. Mentally bottoming out, I decide to go to bed and just curl up in a ball with my dogs by my side and my tears on my pillow. I leave the pills in the bottle—I have to choose between no sleep and oversleeping and just can't take the risk of what the county might do if I miss my reporting time. God, please be with me.

CHAPTER 18

DAY 10: Melissa and I are rattled when we get to my truck after such a tough weekend. Neither one of us has slept. Original plans for a breakfast to celebrate completing the weekend and facing only one last evening inside are quickly abandoned when I end up on the wrong freeway, disoriented from stress and lack of sleep. By the time we get back on track, it's clear that I need to get Melissa home immediately so that she can get ready for her morning class. After dropping her off, I sob the rest of the way home. I am physically and mentally exhausted. I can't believe that I still have one more night in that hell hole.

The few hours that I have at home to launder my clothes, feed and walk my dogs, and re-group go by way too fast. In a strange twist, I am looking forward to tonight for the sole purpose of slamming the door on this miserable experience, once and for all. I am still haunted by dread and anxiety, but knowing that my ordeal is almost over strengthens my resolve. I've got to pull it together and think this through. I will be discharged at the Intake/Process Out Building, which is about two miles away from Tent City's parking area. If I park in the jail lot rather than the Intake Building, I will either have to walk or take a taxi to get to my vehicle. One way or the other, I am going to have to travel that distance without my truck. I'd rather do it now, so that tomorrow, when I am released, I can just get in the truck and go.

Preparing for my last evening at the "nightclub" has me much more jittery than usual. My routine—dressing in my jail clothes and packing my cooler—suddenly becomes confusing. Like I'm doing this for the first time. My racing mind is jumbled with random thoughts and images. I need to calm down and focus or I will surely do something to set me back. I am so close to finishing … Focus! I decide to take a Xanax to mellow out and, after I park tonight, I will swallow my Ambien. Setting out both pills on the bathroom counter, I step away to the kitchen to get a bottled water. If I skip the smuggling tonight, I can just concentrate on getting myself there and home with little else to worry about. Returning to the bathroom sink I look down and notice that the Xanax is there, but the Ambien is missing. Panicking at not being able to remember whether I've taken the Ambien, and knowing that I have a long drive ahead of me as well as a long night, I decide to make myself sick. There isn't much in my belly and I'm not sure if the pill has already dissolved. A few minutes and stomach-heaves later, I find the Ambien on the floor. It either rolled off the counter or I somehow knocked it off as I walked out. What is wrong with me tonight? I'm losing it. Recalling if I opened my mouth to take a pill two minutes ago suddenly becomes a challenge. I'm a mess. I take several deep breaths, grab my things, and head out the door to get Melissa.

The final ride to The Tent is silent. For me it is the unknown of processing out, and for Melissa it is the separation anxiety and fear of not having me with her during her remaining five days of confinement. We have been joined at the hip over the last ten days, which has helped make the time less lonely and fearful. We have looked out for each other like siblings in a new city. In the days ahead Melissa will not only have to find someone to take her back and forth from jail, but she will, in all likelihood, keep to herself, making the evenings feel much longer than they already are.

We arrive at intake and see that the "nice guard" is on duty. Thank goodness. She actually treats us like human beings and even engages us in small talk from time to time. I glance down at the table where we lay our belongings and notice a Ziploc bag of candy. Wondering if one of the work release inmates tried sneaking it in, I ask the guard whose candy it is. She laughs and says, "One of the ladies brought me some candy as a gift. You all know why you guys can't bring that stuff in, don't ya? It's so Sheriff Joe can make money off you!" She smiles and continues processing us in as I nod my head in understanding. She has confirmed what I thought from the start. Granted, it was said tongue-in-cheek by a guard who probably isn't privy to the accounting practices of the county's penitentiary system. Still, I can feel my blood begin to boil. I should be angry with myself for allowing my emotions to get the better of me, but I can't get past my frustration over the corruption within the system. In for the last time, I am consumed by all the different profit centers entangled within the web woven by the Sheriff's department.

Melissa and I head straight for our bunks to get settled in, brush our teeth and sit down for a chat with Mob Mom. She immediately goes into the story about Carlie and this morning's interaction with Carlie's husband, who was waiting for her after we all were released. It turns out that Mob Mom told Carlie's husband that Carlie arrived for check-in stinking of booze and was rolled up and put in stripes, so she won't need a ride this morning. Apparently, Carlie blew a 0.15, which is certainly more than a glass of wine at lunch. It didn't surprise her husband; he just rolled his eyes and shared that Carlie is a full-blown alcoholic and needs help. So sad. The situation made me begin to think about all the families that have been broken apart by alcoholism. I imagine some states give DUI offenders a slap on the wrist—perhaps a fine and probation—allowing alcoholics to hide their affliction and brush off the DUI as an isolated event. Here in Arizona, you face your sins head on. Whether you are an alcoholic who got caught driving or someone who made a bad decision one day, a major family disruption called jail time forces you to examine in much greater detail what you've done and why it happened.

The tent is still buzzing with activity, but I just want to find a way to make morning arrive as fast as possible. Setting an alarm is futile. There's no telling when they will call for kick-outs in the morning. I am assured by my tent mates that if I don't hear my name called, the guards will wake me up. I have been forewarned that processing-out is one of the three worst parts of The Tent experience. One last chance to get inside your head, I guess. If it's anything like the initial intake process, I will need psychotherapy after this is all over. My stomach is in knots and I wonder if I'll be able to fall asleep, even with all of the medication running through my veins. After nine nights here, I have settled into the routine of the tents and, for the most part, know what's expected of me. Tonight and into the morning will be different. The unknown is terrifying and intimidating.

Wiping the sleep from my eyes, I lean over to look at the clock and see that it reads 11:08 p.m. I thank a couple of the ladies for waking me, because I didn't hear my name and bunk number called. A whopping two hours of sleep and immediately my heart begins to race. Sitting up on the side of my bunk, I pause for a moment to get my bearings and compile a list of things to do. First thing—head to the bathroom. My linens need to be packed up and somehow I have to carry them and my personal stuff to the administration area. The day ... Well, night has come. It's time to leave this rat hole and I am nothing short of euphoric. I say my goodbyes to many of my bunk mates with hugs and smiles. Some manage to smile back and watch as I prepare my things; others just turn back to their bunks for the little bit of sleep they can manage to get between interruptions.

Walking toward the office with all my things, I savor the serenity of the darkness. Having never been awake at this time of night inside the confines, I take a moment to enjoy the silence—no guards harassing and making comments, no sinister stares from other inmates, and the absence of some unidentifiable stench in the air. Just as I am approaching the office and beginning to break into a smile suggestive of a very small appreciation for this place, my aura is interrupted by a guard's voice: "Throw your linens in a pile over there and wait here." I am quickly reminded that I'm still inside and, as long as this remains the case, there will be no peace.

There are six of us being released this morning. I watch as two of the girls get handcuffed in front of me; my hands are cuffed quickly thereafter. Once everyone is in cuffs, we are cuffed again in pairs. Seriously? Why in God's name would we do anything to jeopardize our final release from this place? If they told me to keep my wrists touching until we are on the outside, I would have gladly done it. Really no need for the steel bracelets. But of course! It dawns on me that this is their last opportunity to impress us, to remind us of our conviction and incarceration. The guards escort us to a big bus, where we are caged and locked in. I imagine a cinematic rollover, a fiery crash where no one can get out because of the handcuffs.

Once we arrive at the building where we will experience the final segment of this horrific experience, we step off the bus and are escorted to the "tank," a room with concrete benches, no windows, and one toilet. By counting the concrete blocks that surround us, I estimate that the cell is approximately six by thirteen feet. It's half-past eleven and the six of us join three others already crammed into the tiny holding cell. After a few Spanish words are exchanged, I find out that the three women were illegally in the U.S. and have been in the cell for over two days waiting to be deported. Two of them are lying on the benches trying to get some sleep. Finding a place to sit in this filthy, smelly, cold concrete room is a challenge. I weasel my way on to a small section of the bench and close my eyes. My bunk space was the Ritz Carlton compared to this. I now wish that I had not taken my nighttime meds. Eyes heavy and strength depleted, I become increasingly aware that I am not going to get any sleep in the tank. Minutes turn into hours.

Every fifteen or twenty minutes the guard opens the door and more inmates come in. The majority of the women in the tank are donning the signature pink-striped outfits and orange rubber slip-on shoes. Now bursting with about forty women ranging in ages from twenty to sixty-five, the tank is surely over-capacity. Still in my seat, I have my legs pressed to my chest and my arms wrapped around my knees. After all, I don't want to step on the girl sitting on the floor directly beneath me. It's so tight in here that one small unintentional bump could trigger a pushing match that would quickly escalate into an all-out girl fight—and all I want to do is close my eyes and have a little quiet time. Impossible. Nonstop talking. Exchanging of stories. I have no choice but to listen. A young girl in stripes being transferred to another jail tells us that when you are in stripes, you actually have to be assigned to work detail. She worked "Sheriff Joe's Canteen," a white minivan I remember seeing outside of the gates, used to cart the vending machine products around the prison. Striped inmates are also responsible for stocking the vending machines—when the guards decide to fill them. A storage facility evidently holds all the vending items, and it is the task of those assigned to this work detail to unpack, haul and load them. It isn't because of a shortage of junk food that the guards often neglect to order the machines filled.

At 2:40 a.m. a guard arrives with a large laundry cart. Calling out names, he chucks the bags one by one into the cell. The inmates themselves have to figure out whose is whose. The stripes are getting their regular clothes back. Told to change into their street clothes and put their prison garb into the bags, the stripes begin undressing. I look up and notice a closed circuit camera in the ceiling of the tank. I'm sure the guards get their kicks from watching. The exposure to half-naked, hygienically challenged female bodies is enough to make me gag. All the bending movements make the space tighter, if that is even possible. Body heat is steadily raising the cell temperature to near sweltering and, with no air circulation, the odor is atrocious. Two of the girls are sitting on the floor with their faces two inches from the toilet seat. Impossible to expect a roomful of women to refrain from using the toilet for an extended period of time. I glance over at a woman dropping her pants and, as the closest inmates try to move, relieving herself over the toilet. I have to pee, but I would rather piss myself than use the toilet. After witnessing a couple of feminine napkin changes, I've about had it. Helpless and at the mercy of the system, I close my teary eyes and just wait it out.

I hear a plethora of charges pridefully spewed about—including underage drinking, DUI, drug possession, parole violations, outstanding warrants, and on and on. One woman is being extradited back to Oregon for child support charges. I am sharing this claustrophobic space with a heroin addict, a stripper, a self-proclaimed high-priced whore, and a meth addict, along with a host of other degenerates. The heroin addict is bragging that one of her "customers" posted her bail and will be picking her up. Okay ... she's an addict and a hooker. Her boyfriend doesn't know what's going on. The girls cannot shut up. Everyone is trying to top one another's stories. Everyone trying to be the center of attention. Baby daddy this, baby daddy that, my old man, my pimp ... SHUT THE FUCK UP. One crazy lady in stripes—greasy hair and missing teeth—keeps asking if someone would give her a ride to Fountain Hills, or even Scottsdale. Scary. The hours are passing painfully slowly. Each time the doors open, a glimmer of hope is extinguished when, instead of releasing anyone, they throw more girls into our tank. Years of therapy might never erase these last traumatic hours. Crazy as it sounds, I am beginning to miss my bunk and my tent mates. Thank God I'm wearing a watch; otherwise it would be so easy to lose track of time.

Finally, the guard calls out a few names. My watch says 5:03 a.m. Three girls leave, but return shortly. They are all being transferred to different jails within the county to serve new sentences. The door opens again at 5:35 a.m. The guard calls about half of us out and orders us into a different, and somehow smaller, tank. No mention of what's happening. It's all just a waiting game. So we wait. The door is left open, allowing us to watch the activity in the hallways and foyers. Guards walk by as the male inmates, in a tank across the hall, pound on the door and yell obscenities. New inmates are being processed in. There are about twenty-five of us in the smaller tank. One by one, names are called until about half of us step out. Not included in this first group, I anxiously watch the process.

I don't think the guard preparing the final paperwork can read or write any slower. It is as if he's mentally challenged. But then I remind myself that it's all a game—another stalling technique to make being here as emotionally draining as possible. The DMV moves at lightning speed compared to this bunch of bureaucrats. I want to go out there and do it myself. The administrator flips through the file, asks a few questions, takes another set of fingerprints—then back to the tank. What should have been completed in a minute is averaging ten minutes per person. The same group is called back out into the hall and instructed to line up against the wall. One by one each girl is called up to a sergeant's desk, asked a few more questions, made to wait while more paperwork is signed, and then instructed to line up against another wall. Finally the last girl finishes the process and lines up with the rest of them. The final instruction: go out through the exit doors, one by one. I can hear screams of joy as they leave the building, hard evidence that we really will be allowed to exit this place—eventually. The rest of us wait patiently, secretly hoping that we will be processed out much faster.

No such luck. I am the third one called out and find that the process is identical to what I saw earlier. As I stand against the wall, eagerly waiting the final moments before being called up to talk to the sergeant and then released, the administrator finishes up with the last girl. Wait for it … Ah … What? Instead of leading us to the exit, a guard takes us back to our holding cell. No explanation. This time the door is closed behind us. We are all angry and confused. At 7 a.m., the door finally opens, but what we hope and pray will be our deliverance turns into a breakfast delivery. The usual—bags of bread and oranges—just like back in The Tent. I can't even look at it. I don't know if I will ever be able to eat another orange as long as I live. I somehow keep it together, even though in my head I am screaming at the top of my lungs. Why the fuck aren't they letting us out? Some girls are worried about their rides or catching their buses, or even making it to work on time. One of the hipster girls stands high on her toes, trying to look out the little window to see what's happening at the desk. Another stalling tactic?

The sergeant is on a breakfast break. Another forty minutes pass and the guard finally opens the door and calls our names. We line up against the wall and wait for the new sergeant to do her thing. A few of the girls are talking, so the sergeant screams out, "Quiet on the wall!" Tormented to the bitter end. Then the final words are spoken: "In a single file, go down the hallway, to the right and leave the building. I don't want to hear any screaming or see any running."

I have never been so excited to see my truck waiting for me in the parking lot. There are also about a half dozen cabs available. It's 7:45 a.m. and I am finally free. With a smile that could light up the sky, I get in to my truck and head home, eager to strip off these filthy jail clothes and shower away the last ten nights.

CHAPTER 19

April 30, 2010: A Few Days After My Release

My pachinko-like emotions leave me wondering about the long-term effects of this experience. The day after my discharge I had to go to work for three days. I kept watching the clock, thinking that I had to be somewhere or that I was forgetting something. The memories have already started to fade, though, and now, many of the details are fuzzy. I'm sure I've forgotten some of them; however, I struggle to forget many of the experiences, such as the evening of kick-out and all the nastiness that transpired over those eight-plus hours. But then, in the same breath, I feel I have lifelong friends in Melissa, Mob Mom, and Grandma Mary. I have been in contact with all three and feel a strange connection to them—more than with other new friendships. Grandma Mary still has twenty-odd days to finish, Melissa was released yesterday, and Mob Mom gets out today … after six months! She's scared about getting settled and rebuilding her life. She and her daughter rented an apartment, and Grandma Mary donated some furniture to get them started.

Last Saturday I helped move some items. It was really

good to see Grandma Mary. We made plans to paint her condo this summer while she is on house arrest. Melissa has to start her thirty-day house arrest today. She is going before the judge to try and get an extension. Between jail, school, community service, and loss of her driver's license, she couldn't find the time to have the special phone line installed that is needed to operate the house arrest system. If it weren't for the damn interlock in my vehicle, I could continue with my life as if nothing happened. Unfortunately, it is a constant reminder.

I understand now how long-term inmates can become "institutionalized." The rigid schedule and routine inside becomes normal. The people you meet are in similar situations, so there is no humiliation or embarrassment. I equate it on one level to the life of doctors and lawyers. (Stay with me on this one.) Every day doctors arrive at work and see sickness everywhere. Every day lawyers deal with lawsuits and law breakers and are surrounded by bookshelves full of case studies. So doctors develop the mentality that the world is in a dire state of sickness and disease and lawyers envision the world as victimized by rampant criminal activity. Similarly, when convicts are incarcerated for long periods of time, they begin to embrace a world based on criminal behavior. Their interaction with other criminals enforces the notion that being part of the community means committing a crime. Everyone speaks openly and freely about their experiences and what they are facing when they get out. It's no surprise that when they do get out and are no longer in this atmosphere, they are uncomfortable. They are surrounded by citizens who look down on them and shun them for their misdoings.

It is rare to find someone inside who will be returning

home to a big house with a picket fence and a loving spouse and children eagerly waiting for a hug and kiss. No … it is much more common to hear horror stories from women returning home to an abusive husband or boyfriend … or from someone who's unsure if she even has a place to go because she's missed rent payments and may have been locked out. Some need to pick up their children from grandma's house; they've lied about their whereabouts during the last ten to thirty days. Still others have been in for so long that they miss the psychological comfort of having a scheduled place to be every night; they will be permanently disturbed by their release into the wild. Once out, they discover that keeping a schedule and hiding the dirty little secret of their incarceration from co-workers, family and friends is an insurmountable challenge.

I have chosen to disclose the details of my experience only in this account. I emailed my family and friends to let them know I am okay, and that I have finished all my obligations—jail and class time, fines. I also told them that right now I choose not to discuss the sordid details and that I hope they will respect my privacy.

I can honestly say that I now understand why people do not want to talk about The Tent. It is so horrible that you just want to forget. As I read through the final manuscript that became this book, I realize that many of the details and stories have already been erased from my memory. Had I not made notes, my story might never have been told.

* * *

On July 6, 2010, Delaware became the eleventh state in 2010 to ban text messaging while driving and the thirtieth state overall to outlaw that offense. The law also makes it illegal to talk on a handheld cell phone while driving. Distracted Driving legislation is sweeping the nation as the use of new technology such as text messaging, tweeting, and electronic book readers become more and more prevalent in all age groups. My reason for mentioning these laws will become strikingly clear as I recount my experience with the state-mandated interlock device for my truck.

My court-ordered enrollment in the ignition interlock program came as no surprise. Not only had I heard about this system, but my attorney told me it was required. Arizona's DOT website paraphrases a study by The International Council on Alcohol, Drugs and Traffic Safety concluding that interlocks, combined with a comprehensive monitoring and service program, lead to a 40 to 95 percent reduction in repeat drunk driving offenses as long as the device remains on the vehicle. Fair enough. It only makes sense that if you have had alcohol and attempt to start a vehicle with an interlock device, it won't start. Obviously that deters driving while intoxicated. I can live with that. What I wasn't prepared for was the other effects it would have on my daily life.

I am still six months away from finishing what has turned out to be a fourteen-month commitment—two months longer than anticipated. The Arizona DMV made an error in my case that it is unwilling to fix. I was told by a DMV employee at the counter that the interlock installation was required before I could get my sixty-day work-only permit; as it turns out, it is only required after the thirty-day hard suspension and sixty-day work-only permit—before you apply for reinstatement of your license. This error cost me another $150 and chained me to this device for two extra months.

I thought this program would become tolerable after I got used to it; I was completely wrong. Take note: BAC levels can remain over legal limits the morning AFTER a night of drinking. It's true and now I have proof. I had one of those nights and kept the truck parked until the morning. I needed to get my truck so that I could get ready for work that afternoon. After accepting a ride from my co-partier of the previous night, I climbed in and attempted to start the ignition. What?? It's reading "FAIL" and sirens are going off—how can that be? Shit … now what? My ride is gone and, knowing that her condition is similar to mine, wouldn't be able to return to help me get my truck home. Panicked, I begin to pace, hoping to come up with a solution. I need to pull myself together and get to work this afternoon. My only option is to call my nephew to come get me.

"Sleeping it off" is a myth. I called the installation service to find out what happens next and was told that I could have blown a low fail or a high fail. The device fails at a minimum of 0.03% BAC, which is considered a low fail, but only a recalibration of the unit can determine my actual BAC level. Fortunately my required monthly calibration is only a few days away. When I take the truck in, they plug the device into a computer that reads EVERYTHING—when I blow, how I blow, when I don't blow or hum enough, and when I fail. At this point, the only critical number I care about is the fail reading.

Well done … I blew a high fail of 0.117% BAC. I was completely floored as to how I could still have been well over the legal limit the morning after. "Because of your body weight," the technician says after giving me a quick visual scan, "you need to be really careful, especially the morning after. We see low and high fails all the time from attempting to drive the morning after a night out." I can't tell you how many times I felt I was being responsible by picking my truck up the morning after a night of drinking. It turns out that I was probably still over the legal limit the following day.

One strike. You are allowed two violations within the year. The third violation will result in an automatic year in addition to the already unreasonable sentence being served. I will never do that again! As I make my appointment and pay for the next calibration, I inquire about the unit and how it affects the car battery. Earlier that month I was having problems with the device. Every time that I blew, it would read "ABORT." According to the manual, that means that you are not blowing or humming enough. Or it could mean there's excessive moisture in the mouthpiece. It suggests waiting ten to twenty seconds and trying again. This was in my own driveway; I was dressed and ready to go to work and couldn't get it to pass. Forty-five minutes later and completely frustrated, I gave up and had to call for a ride to work.

The next time it happens, I am in the parking lot of a home improvement store, with my two dogs in the truck. It is 110 degrees outside, and once again, I get the "ABORT" reading. When I call the installation company, they tell me that it is probably because of my vehicle battery. The battery has to have a certain amount of voltage for the device to work properly. A new $150 battery later and a little humiliation (the AAA technician sees that I have interlock on my vehicle) and I'm once again mobile. I'm furious now. This device continues to cost me over and above the price of the installation and rent.

At my next calibration appointment, I have an intense conversation with the installers. After I explain my recent experience, they tell me, "The device draws a constant slow trickle from the battery. It's necessary to drive your vehicle a minimum of thirty minutes per day, every day, in order for it not to drain your battery."

"I travel for a living, and sometimes I don't drive for days," I tell him, frustrated that this whole interlock experience is draining my battery, bank account, and patience. As I look him in the eyes, I let out my frustration: "Does this mean that in another eight months I am going to have to replace my battery again?"

"Probably so."

"Well that's a BULLSHIT system!"

He is clearly offended. Disgusted that I have allowed myself to fly off the handle about something I can't control, I leave there with my tail between my legs, embarrassed about my high fail and my abusive language.

A week later, I am house-sitting and having a friend over for dinner and wine. No big deal, right? I've learned my lesson and realize I have to allow my small frame plenty of time to absorb last night's wine. Loading my dogs up the next day for a quick afternoon run, I've done the math in my head; thirteen hours ago was the last time I had a drink. When I blow, very much to my surprise, a "warning" light goes off. My vehicle starts anyway. I'm not sure what "warning" means. Nervous that I may have just registered another fail, I call the company.

"Did you have any alcohol today or last evening?"

"Yes, but that was thirteen hours ago."

"Turn off your vehicle and wait a couple of hours, just in case you start driving down the road and during your intermittent blow it registers over 0.02% ... otherwise you could have a 'fail while driving.' That is considered the worst violation under the interlock program and would tack on an additional year." I turn off the truck, drink a lot of water, and wait two more hours. This does the trick and I am cleared to go. One more reminder of my dysfunctional lifestyle that's going to have to change.

It doesn't end there. One sunny afternoon in September, I experience another frustrating event tied to the interlock device. First of all, I understand the purpose of activating the device with a qualifying blow before a vehicle start-up, but I am struggling with the rationale for the periodic BAC re-check while driving. The distraction of having to blow and read the device while in motion is as dangerous as texting while driving or using a cell phone behind the wheel. Has the Arizona DOT or any other state that mandates the interlock program considered this device as a distraction and thus outlawed its use? This is rhetorical question, for obvious reasons. A state cannot possibly mandate the program and, in the same breath, outlaw its use. The hypocrisy is glaringly evident. On this fateful day, while driving on the city streets of Scottsdale, I am requisitioned by the device, with two high-pitch beeps and a flashing red light, to provide a re-test blow. This occurs randomly within the first minutes of driving and then randomly within the next fifteen to forty-five minutes. If you ignore the first warning, a second one follows, this time with a louder beeping. If the test is not completed successfully within six minutes of the first warning, a violation will be recorded. There is really no safe way to complete the test while driving, so I just do the best I can in the time allotted. I feel around in the truck to find the device, give it what I think is a qualifying blow, and get an "ABORT" reading. I'm approaching a car stopped at a red light as I look down at the unit in my right hand to find out what has gone wrong. When I look back up, I slam on my brakes and run into the guy in front of me. Distracted by the device in my hand—which is trying to tell me something—I end up in a collision. Fucking great. All I need is an accident on my record and to have my insurance either skyrocket or be dropped altogether. I get out and look at the damage to both vehicles. My truck is fine; the guy's car has some damage but fortunately he is unhurt. What complicates things is that the other driver doesn't speak a lick of English. I get my housekeeper's daughter, who's bilingual, on my speaker phone and ask her to interpret my questions.

"Do you want me to call the police?"

"¿Quieres que llame a la policía?" she asks him over my cell phone.

"La policía no, no, no. No quiero ser deportados."

His response is easy enough to understand. Apparently he is here illegally and is afraid that if the police get involved, he will be deported. To end the matter quickly, I give him $60 for the damage and we part ways.

I'm sure the stories won't end here. I have to live with this device for several more months and I've only related a few of the unpleasant and inconvenient consequences to date. It should now be clear why I opened up this chapter with the latest in Distracted Driving legislation. The interlock program needs either to change its equipment to be less distracting or improve the re-test process. Doing nothing trades impairment for distraction, neither of which belongs on our roads.

CHAPTER 20

One Year Later

That fateful day in November of 2009 has left its mark on my life in many ways, directly and indirectly.

My therapist tells me that, difficult as it may be, it's good to remember the emotional pain and stress of my ordeal—so that I will never again be tempted to take those same risks that brought the law down upon my head. I try to look at it as a learning experience and an opportunity to warn others about the significant repercussions of poor judgment and behavior. I've become much more aware of my bad habits and sometimes reckless behavior, but until now I have been too afraid to share—afraid of more embarrassment and humiliation. Instead of trying to teach others, I simply remind the people I'm having a drink with that they should call a cab and leave it at that. I don't want to become known as an expert in DUIs or some righteous bitch. Individuals need to make their own decisions about risk and responsibility, live by them, and accept the consequences.

My way of life has changed. My experience left me financially devastated, physically exhausted, and mentally and emotionally detached from all things that existed before.

The treatment received on the inside is supposed to deter inmates from ever repeating their criminal behavior. For the most part, this holds true. At least for me. However, memories fade. Your stay in Tent City strengthens your resolve, and you leave with the impression that you'll never face anything worse than this. If you make it though and come up against another similar situation, you now know that you will survive. Repeat offenders are on the rise and I think it's because of this reasoning.

Force offenders to tolerate the intolerable and, after they prevail, they will become invincible—at least in their own minds. Able to handle another conviction … unafraid of what lies ahead because it's now known …

I'm not implying that jails should be cushy. I just believe that the overplayed tough-guy routine is getting unwarranted praise from the press. Clearly the public wants to believe that heaping misery and resentment on people who drink irresponsibility will scare them straight.

Experience has taught me the opposite.

And more than a few of those who believe in our punitive prison system might be advised to remind themselves: "There but for the grace of God, go I."

AFTERWORD

On Drinking and Driving

I am no longer speaking on behalf of the woman whose story I have related, but as myself, Mark Feuerer.

Few personal experiences trigger permanent changes in behavior and attitude. Falling in love, becoming a parent for the first time, discovering that a loved one has a terminal illness or coping with the premature death of a friend or family member … I include a DUI conviction in this category. It is an attitude-altering, behavior-modifying event that, in the worst case, sends you to jail for manslaughter and, best case, involves you in lengthy court proceedings. Both these results exact a hefty financial toll and should inspire a prompt re-evaluation of one's personal choices.

I've done it. You've likely done it at some point in your life and if you haven't, you know someone who has. Driving under the influence of alcohol and/or drugs is probably the most culturally important violation of a law, and I'm willing to bet that it's more common than any other in the world. What makes DUIs so prevalent and yet so abhorrent is the fact that in virtually every case, they are unintentional. Drunk drivers, and most of the population, believe that *being caught* while driving under the influence is the crime. Conversely, not getting caught—making it to your destination without incident—is legal in some strange way. If a shoplifter walks out of a store with a purse full of stolen jewelry and isn't caught, the shoplifter still realizes a crime was committed.

It is "intention" that differentiates between these two crimes. My limited law school instruction defines criminal intent in two categories, "specific" and "general" (or "basic"), with two requirements in question: acting knowingly and acting with a specific purpose in mind. DUIs are "general intent" crimes because the prosecutor need only prove the act of driving under the influence; that act alone breaks the law. The intention to break the law does not come into play. "Specific" intent requires both elements to be present—the act and the intention. One could argue that a DUI offender, knowing he has been drinking and is probably over the legal limit for driving, is knowingly breaking the law. However, that point is difficult to prove, given the effects of drugs and alcohol on the mental state of the offender. Therefore, it is typically prosecuted as a "general intent" crime. Other "general intent" crimes are rape and manslaughter.

A more thorough definition of this crime is "knowingly driving with a diminished ability to do so and still choosing to take the risk of causing injury to another or oneself, whether physically or to their property while driving intoxicated." The mentality, "It's not a crime if I don't hurt anybody," is all too common for DUI offenders. No one sets out at the beginning of an evening with plans to get drunk and drive around maliciously, hoping to cause an accident or an injury to another without getting caught. Yet when the morning rolls around, the drunk driver inevitably wakes up to two important observations: the night before (s)he was drunk and (s)he drove home. Conscientious people regret the combination, but still too many make it a part of their weekly activities without so much as second-guessing their decision to drive.

I was recently reading a book titled *Holiness by Grace*, by Bryan Chapell, and came across this statement: "Common to our humanity are the flaws that make us all susceptible to such terrible and potentially tragic errors." As human beings, we live in a fallen world and are flawed—never rising above making mistake after mistake right up until the day we are called home. Recognizing that we are helpless in the face of temptation, we all need to find repentance and heal our relationship with God.

My days of driving under the influence have ended and, looking back at those periods in my life, I truly regret my behavior. As late as the mid-'80s, DUI was still considered a crime difficult to enforce without an adequate number of police department staff to manage the process. My little home town had several bars that catered to twenty-somethings and, even more so, marketed the idea of cheap beer and cocktails with the hope of selling both in quantity. There were no cabs waiting to take people home and no police waiting outside at closing time hoping to catch DUI offenders. The designated driver program would begin at the end of the night as our group of guys would collectively decide who was the least impaired. Most assumed that if they could walk out of the establishment with a portion of their faculties still intact, they could get themselves home untarnished. This went on weekend after weekend, and everyone seemed content with the system. The small town would even host an annual festival next to the high school where beer and wine flowed freely outdoors during softball games. Police were around for crowd control and ready to step in when a couple of over-served knuckleheads would begin to poke each other in the chests with their index fingers. Still, with no cabs waiting to take them home, festival attendees would climb into their vehicles, hassle-free, and drive off.

In the early '90s, things began to change. Friends were getting DUIs. Some more than one. The penalties back then were minor—a fine of around $500, some mandatory class hours, a few points taken away. For a first offense, jail time was waived. Awareness that DUI enforcement was becoming more prevalent began to seep into the minds of the entire troop. Our sense of responsibility was heightened and as we aged and began families, the level of intoxication lessened along with the decision to drive afterward. The behavior didn't entirely disappear, however. It would take many years of maturity coupled with the morning effect of the previous night's hard drinking to spur real behavioral changes among the clan. I suspect that the behavior of our circle of friends was common across state lines during this time. We were very lucky none of us injured or killed anyone or were killed ourselves.

The death tolls across the country from DUI-related accidents were increasing at alarming rates and activism born in the early '80s was starting to gain momentum.

Mothers Against Drunk Driving (M.A.D.D.), the first organization I remember having a voice on this subject, was founded in 1980 by a mother whose daughter was killed by a drunk driver in California. The early '80s were a developmental time for this organization, but it took a tragedy in Kentucky for a substantial number of people to support this organization and bolster its membership.

I remember one Sunday morning in particular: the night before, a drunk driver had headed down the wrong side of a freeway and collided with a church bus, killing twenty-seven people and injuring many others. On this historically significant weekend, I was a senior in college celebrating the completion of my thesis. Although saddened by the news, I was a student with no connection yet to the real, working world; I barely made a connection between my own behavior and that of the drunk driver.

Many years later, I was visiting my mother at our childhood home. She asked me to go out to the garage to see what she had run over the night before when pulling her car in after a night out with friends. As I opened the garage door I was immediately taken aback by the front of the car partially sticking out the back of the garage. Not only had she misdiagnosed the accident, but she hadn't even realized that she had knocked out a portion of the garage wall with her vehicle. My mother passed away a couple of years ago and by all accounts—save this one—she was an incredible woman. A devout Christian, active in her church, and the matriarch of our very large, eight-sibling family. She had more love and devotion to family and God in her left pinky than I could ever hope for in my whole body. A model citizen—honest, trustworthy, responsible, and above all else, forgiving. I could easily go on and on, but you get the picture. If a woman such as this one could occasionally show such terrible judgment, then it can happen to anyone who ever takes a drink.

Tent City, Arizona

Now that you are familiar with the term "Tent City" as it applies to Arizona, you may be thinking that you've heard this name before. In third world nations and some upscale U.S. cities such as Sacramento and Seattle, "Tent City" refers to a shanty town. These homeless areas are made up of actual nylon tents and cardboard boxes; for the "lucky" ones, pallets and rusted corrugated steel roofs are the shelters of choice— as if they had a choice. As during the Great Depression of the 1920s and in poor, undeveloped or underdeveloped nations, survival is a way of life and possessions are few.

Arizona's Tent City is notably different: the claim is that it deters crime.

Arizona makes the news fairly regularly—as a destination for northerners during the winter months, and because of baseball's spring training and immigration control. It also houses the most compelling and controversial sheriff's office in the nation. Five-term Sheriff Joe Arpaio has been an international public figure in law enforcement since he re-introduced "chain-gangs"—phased out as a form of acceptable punishment in 1955—to the incarcerated and, in 1993, built a prison known as Tent City, encompassing tens of acres and boarding 2,000 inmates. There's a fine line between "extreme" and "excessive," and I believe Sheriff Arpaio and his posse dance along it every day.

Personally, I am a big fan of what he's doing here in Maricopa County. His efforts to fight crime—saving taxpayer money and publicly humiliating those who have stepped over state legal boundaries as a deterrent—are as unique as they are fascinating. While raising the flag for "Sheriff Joe," I question the effectiveness of the deterrence. His website says he's reducing crime with his style of enforcement and, on the surface, his tactics appear to be working. Data provided in Maricopa County public records indicate otherwise. If statistics bore you, skip to the end, but take away this one possibility: the Arpaio system is broken. However, if you're like me and need proof backed by data, let's examine the numbers.

First, let's assume that those committing crimes prompted by stupidity and/or ignorance are doing it without really knowing or understanding the potentially severe consequences of getting caught. Yeah, they are aware that jail awaits slow and dim-witted criminals; only they do not believe this group includes them. While Arpaio's methodologies have been repeatedly touted by the media, they don't take into account the immutability of the criminal mindset. The notion that "it will never happen to me" or "Tent City can't be that bad" sticks to their consciousness like feathers on tar. And criminals aren't the only ones who think this way.

While year-to-year data on population fluctuations in Maricopa County is difficult to obtain, the latest data from a county census taken in 2005 shows a population of 3,700,516. As of July 2008, the estimate is 3,954,598—an increase of 6.4%. Census data taken in 2010—and likely not available to the public for another year—will provide actual numbers of how population has increased or perhaps decreased from 2005 to 2010. Until these numbers come out, we will use the 6.4% increase in population as the basis for comparison.

With this in mind, let's move on to some interesting Maricopa County statistics published on the Arizona Department of Public Safety's website. From 2005–2008, total arrests (ranging from breaking curfew to murder) of people under the age of eighteen went up by 23 percent and the total for all ages eighteen and over went up 17 percent. Only for one age group, twenty-four-year-olds, did arrests increase at a slower rate (5.2 percent) than the overall population during the same time period. Otherwise, arrests for all other age groups increased between 10 percent and a whopping 38 percent (fifty-five to fifty-nine-year-olds). If someone has a logical explanation for why people in their late fifties are committing crimes at increasingly alarming rates, I'd love to hear it.

Back to the statistics. One might argue that petty infractions such as breaking curfew should be removed from these statistics. Okay, let's take a look at just the worst crimes, ranging from arson to murder (a "Part I" offense classification in Maricopa County) during this same time period. It is *up a staggering 13 percent for all age groups*. These increases suggest a correlation between an increase in criminal behavior and Arpaio's incarceration methods.

How can this increase be explained?

The Maricopa County Sheriff's department will likely tell you that more personnel and aggressive tactics on the street lead to more arrests. They even suggest that crimes by repeat offenders have tapered off because of their experiences in The Tent. An article written for the Intellectual Conservative Arizona website in September of 2008 (no one person is taking credit for ownership of this blog, hence no mention of authorship) argues that the number of repeat offenders sent to prison in Maricopa County is setting records. So there you have it: there are a record number of repeat offenders (if you can believe the blogged information), and data clearly states that the number of arrests has increased. Additionally, the number of drug-related DUI cases handled by the Arizona Department of Public Safety rose from about 4,400 in 1999 to more than 14,700 last year—an increase of more than 230 percent. The state's population in that period rose about 38 percent (JJ Hensley—Apr. 8, 2010 12:00 a.m., *The Arizona*

Republic).

The specialized incarceration system currently in place to specifically deter criminal acts appears—based on the above data—not to be working.

Either the "Arpaio" system isn't an effective means to deter crime or the word on Tent City is not getting out to those thinking about committing crimes or those who continue to drink and drive. I believe that the latter is true, and that is my primary reason for bringing this information to you.

The risks we take bring knee-buckling consequences. This is especially true in Arizona. In addition, citizens outside Arizona shouldn't be ignoring these facts or pointing fingers, whether or not they plan to visit Arizona. These methods of deterrence are making major news because of their positive effects on Arizona's state budget. In all likelihood they will soon be adopted by other states seeking a financial boost.

Clearly, fifteen-cent inmate meals and free roadside cleanup are good for a state's economy. However, are chain gangs and tent cities really what you want for your town or county? Do we really want to balance the state budget on the backs of criminals and people who make bad choices—even if that punishment does nothing to keep them from reoffending in the future? Indeed, the present system is so punitive that it often leaves offenders with nothing to lose.

As in the story recounted on these pages, the "reformed offender" is left with post-traumatic stress, a new social circle of shady characters, and a crushing pile of bills. I do not believe that the woman who told me her story will ever drink and drive again. I'm willing to bet she's one of the exceptions.

Mark Feuerer was born and raised in Menomonee Falls, Wisconsin, a small town just northwest of Milwaukee. He is the youngest of eight siblings. Mark headed off to Princeton University in 1984, where he played baseball, football and graduated with a B.A. in Psychology. After a short stint playing professional baseball in Australia in 1989-1990, he settled into a career in the heavy construction equipment industry, working on both the manufacturing and dealership sides of the business. He received his MBA in 1998 from Keller Graduate School of Management and spent 2003 in law school at New England School of Law. In 2008, he married his wife Kelly (nee Weigand), managing attorney for a healthcare network provider. Mark, Kelly, and their three cats and one dog live in Scottsdale, Arizona.

Mark's reasons for writing this book are two-fold. First, he's been in a vehicle when a DUI arrest was made and second, he feels fortunate to have escaped being caught breaking this law when it wasn't a big issue several years back. He has certainly changed his ways. Hearing this story from a long-time acquaintance inspired him to get the word out about the consequences of drinking and driving. Having once worked for a car service, he's driven home many inebriated customers. Although glad to see that some people are making wise choices, he knows that far too many are still getting behind the wheel after drinking. He hopes this book will make a difference.